Greensleeves
Garden-Lover's Guide to Southern England

Compiled by: James Lawrence, Robin Morris, Mervyn Woodward   Edited by: James Lawrence

CONTENTS

Published by:
Bracken Publishing, Bracken House, 199a Holt Road, Cromer, Norfolk NR27 9JN

ISBN 1 871614 21 X

Printed by: Broadgate Printers, Industrial Est., Aylsham, Norwich.
November 1994

IMPORTANT

Please note:-

1. Every effort is made to ensure accuracy, but inevitably errors and onissions may occur.
Therefore the publisher cannot accept liability for any consequences arising therefrom.

2. Prices, where quoted, may alter during the currency of this guide.

3. SUNDAY OPENING: new laws mean that many establishments may open only for six hours on a Sunday.
We have ensured opening hours are as up-to-date as possible, but if you are in any doubt
you are advised to telephone your destination in advance.

4. It is not claimed that every good garden centre or garden is featured.
The editor would welcome correspondence, favourable or not, concerning gardens or garden centres
you have visited ANYWHERE ON THE BRITISH MAINLAND that are not in the following pages.
All letters will be gratefully acknowledged, and those which prove most useful will be awarded a
COMPLIMENTARY COPY of the next edition.

Free Book

The editor also welcomes correspondence concerning INNS & PUBS, HOTELS & RESTAURANTS,
for use in forthcoming editions of our Trencherman's Guides.
All letters will be gratefully acknowledged, and all those which prove useful will be awarded a
complimentary copy of the new edition, at the discretion of the editor.

From the Same Publisher

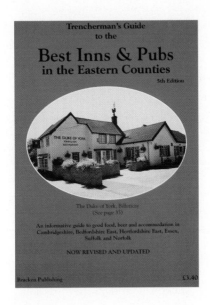

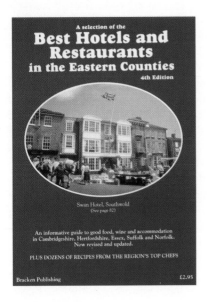

Available from most bookshops and many of the pubs, hotels and restaurants themselves, within region;
or direct from publisher in writing, enclosing payment of £3.50 per book, to include p&p.

TREBAH GARDEN
Mawnan Smith, nr Falmouth.
Tel: (01326) 250448
Fax: (01326) 250781

"This is no pampered, pristine, prissy garden with rows of clipped hedges, close-mown striped lawns and daily raked paths. You are going to see a magnificent, old, wild and magical Cornish garden – the end product of 100 years of inspired and dedicated creation, followed by 40 years of mellowing and 10 years of love and restoration." So reads the introduction to the official guide, obviously written with a fierce pride. And few would challenge these assertions.

Trebah stands at the head of a 25-acre ravine, over 500 yards long and dropping 250ft to the glorious Helford estuary. The ravine is flanked by giant rhododendrons, many planted in the last century, a riot of colour in season. There are a number of paths to take you down to the beach (where one is welcome to swim or picnic); look for the Water Garden and the Zig-Zag, planted with a rare and beautiful collection of exotic plants, mainly from the Mediterranean. There are so many diversions: Camellia Walk, the Koi Pool, Mallard Pond, the Chusan Palms (said to be the tallest in England), but you will be

followed everywhere by luscious fragrances, and be presented at every turn by the most wonderful aspect.

The garden and beach make for a marvellous day out with the family, and children will love Tarzan's Camp (enclosed within a giant tree canopy with ropes, climbing frames and slides), the Paraglide for over-fives, and the 'Trebah Trails' for young and old. There is also a garden shop which sells light refreshments. Dogs are permitted on leads.

After your visit you may be tempted to join the Garden Trust, formed by the Hibbert family in 1987 – details from the shop or enquire direct.

Open: Daily from 10:30am, last admission 5pm.

PROBUS GARDENS
Probus, nr Truro.
Tel: (01726) 882597
Fax: (01726) 883868

Described by BBC Gardener's World as "an inspiration," Probus Gardens are much more than a stunning display of plants and garden designs. They comprise one of only five centres of excellence established nationwide with the specific purpose of helping visitors to get more out of their own gardens.

Cornwall County Council set up these demonstration showcase gardens in 1969 in a meadow situated mid-way between St Austell and Truro on the A390, astride the backbone of Cornwall. Probus has become Mecca for those who love gardening and is said to be the source of some of the most expert advice available in the region.

Yet in 1993 the gardens were faced with closure, until public pressure held sway. Since then they have flourished, with record numbers of visitors enjoying the unique facilities. In part that renaissance has come from the painstaking work put in on the seven-acre site. Curator Alistair Rivers and his dedicated team have shown what can be accomplished in a typical Cornish garden . . . then gone on to demonstrate what can be achieved with imagination and the cunning use of hedging. The result is a series of differing sub-climates and dazzling array of literally thousands of species. For an example of the rich diversity, a "wind-tender" garden, created using exotic plants which would normally perish in such conditions, is currently under construction just a few paces away from desert and hardy exotic gardens.

The continual trials of gardening techniques make Probus unique, and visitors can discover new ideas for themselves. There also many arts and crafts courses held here. Whatever your reason for a visit, you are likely to find something to inspire you.

The entry fee at time of writing is £2.25 for adults, children under 16 free. Groups and coach parties welcome. Details and gardening advice can be obtained free by phoning or writing to Alistair Rivers.

OPEN: Easter to Sept. 10am to 5pm daily; Oct. to Easter 10am to 4:30pm Mon - Fri.

HELIGAN MANOR GARDENS

Pentewan, nr St Austell.
Tel: (01726) 844157
Fax: (01726) 843023

"If you only visit one garden this year, then make sure it's Heligan. If you want to see two, come twice!" This exuberant, tongue-in-cheek invitation is extended on the front of a publicity leaflet, but what is going on here is quite extraordinary: no less than "The garden restoration of the century" (George Plumptre, The Times).

As recently as 1990 the 100-acre site was a wreck, neglected for years and further devastated by hurricane winds. Progress could only be made by machete. From the unlikely background of record producer and archaeologist, Tim Smit has joined with local builder John Nelson and wrought a staggering transformation. In doing so they have revealed late 18th- and early 19th-century techniques which have largely been forgotten. They have the considerable advantages of a benificent microclimate and spectacular topography, which together have created a kind of sub-tropical Shangri-la in this corner of England.

One of the most spectacular features is a ravine (with cave), water cascading through four pools: ideal for ferns. Water also flows through "The Jungle," in a steep valley which has the best collection of tree ferns in Britain, a well as 40 varieties of bamboo and the three largest species of tree in the country. It defies belief that the large vegetable garden was, as late as December 1992, under 15ft of brambles and trees. Other wonders include the oldest type of tree in the world (250 million years!), perhaps the biggest rhododendron in the world at 86ft, a crystal grotto, wishing well, Italian garden, flower garden, sundial garden, "New Zealand" (oddly with no plants from that country), bee boles, melon house, banana house and countless rarities introduced by Victorian plant hunters. In two very fine walled gardens are a pineapple pit and exotic fruit houses.

The excitement of those involved in the project is understandable, and anyone with a taste for the romance of discovery should not miss "The Lost Gardens of Heligan" (which means "Willow').

OPEN: 10am to 6pm (last admission 4:30pm) every day (allow two hours to see it). Stout footwear recommended. Dogs permitted on leads. Tearoom. Plant sales. Large sections of garden suitable for disabled. Guided tours bookable for 12 or more.

TREWITHEN GARDENS
Grampound Road, Truro.
Tel: (01726) 882763/4
Fax: (01726) 882301

Trewithen is Cornish for 'the House in the Spinney', appropriate enough back in 1904, when George Johnstone, who was responsible for much of what we see today, inherited the estate. His forebears had, over two centuries, planted many fine trees; indeed, it was necessary for Johnstone to thin them out in order to give other plants a chance.

World War I was responsible for the felling of 300 beeches (by government order), but it allowed Johnstone an opportunity to create the wonderful glade which still stretches southwards over 200 yards from the front of the house. Flanking both sides are rarities from all over the world, but especially Asia, collected from the wild by botanical expeditions of the 19th and early 20th centuries.

Camellias are very much a forte, including C. 'Donation' from which all the others in the world have been taken. There is also a great variety of magnolias, hosts of rhododendrons (including the marvellous yellow R. macabeanum, said to be the finest specimen in the Western World), and many birches and maples.

There is much else besides in the 28 acres, including an admirable walled garden. Allow at least two hours for a tour, and be sure to pick up the attractive little guide book, with a map and colour photos. There is also a video presentation, plus PLANT CENTRE, TEA SHOP picnic and play area.

Open: 1st March to 30th September, Mon to Sat 10am - 4:30pm, plus Sundays in April & May. House open 2pm to 4pm on Mons & Tues only from April to July.

PENCARROW
Washaway, nr Bodmin.
Tel: (01208) 841369

These privately owned 50-acre historic gardens were laid out during the second quarter of the 19th century by statesman Sir William Molesworth, often using seeds brought from China or western America by the great plant hunters of the day. One famous contributor was William Lobb, who was actually born here and who introduced the monkey-puzzle tree, named in these gardens by Charles Austin, a noted parliamentary lawyer.

Approach the house by a mile-long drive flanked by huge specimen conifers, rhododendrons and camellias, specialities of these gardens. Admire the formal sunken Italian Garden in front of the mansion, and the great granite rockery constructed with vast blocks carted from Bodmin Moor. Follow the path along the stream to the lake, and on to the Woodland American Gardens.

These were originally planted only with species from the Americas, but now this sheltered valley is home to many of the 600 different hybrid rhododendrons and 200 types of conifer planted by the present owner, Sir Arscott Molesworth-St Aubyn.

Then stroll back through the park and visit the PLANT SHOP or CRAFT CENTRE. Have a rest over a light lunch whilst watching the children in the play area, and conclude a very pleasant day out with a tour round the superbly appointed family home, still lived-in. Sir Arthur Sullivan composed 'Iolanthe' during a stay here in 1882. In season you could pick-your-own soft fruit.

OPEN: gardens dawn until dusk daily through the season; house, tearooms and craft centre 1:30pm to 5pm Sunday to Thursday, from Easter to 15th October. 1st June to 10th Sept. & Bank Hol. Mons open 11am.

DUCHY OF CORNWALL NURSERIES

Penlyne Cott Road, Lostwithiel.
Tel: (01208) 872668
Fax: (01579) 345672

It is not only the royal connection (Prince Charles is Duke of Cornwall) that marks this 12-acre nursery as special; it is a lovely spot for a stroll and to picnic, and it is one of the country's leading centres for rare plants – enquiries come in from far and wide. The friendly staff are always eager to share their considerable knowledge. They need to be versatile, for they sell a full range: conifers, shrubs, roses, perennials, fruit trees, aquatics, houseplants and much more, and in so many varieties – not just one type of buddliea, but 20, for example. Having started in 1970 as a forestry nursery, trees are still a speciality, as are coastal plants and those suitable for milder areas. Yet for all this, prices are most competitive.

There is a move to organic methods, employing natural pest controls which include a cat on the payroll to keep down rodents!

OPEN: 9am - 5pm, Mon to Sat, 10am - 5pm Sun. Bookshop and information desk. Closed Bank Hols.

MOUNT EDGCUMBE HOUSE & GARDENS

Cremyll, Torpoint.
Tel: (01752) 822236
Fax: (01752) 822199

In a region that can justifiably boast some of the world's finest gardens, Mt Edgcumbe stands out as a national treasure. The house and many points within its 800 acres command dramatic views over Plymouth Sound, and would have witnessed the English fleet sailing out to join battle with the Spanish Armada. Its commander, Admiral Medina Sidonia, may have regretted his prophecy that he would soon be living there. Presumably Hitler entertained no such ambition, for his bombers did manage to inflict serious damage to the House, but it was rebuilt faithfully to the original plan.

Now in less troubled times we can all enjoy the marvels of this very special place. One could pick over the many coves and inlets, wander by the lakes or through the woodland paths (you may espy fallow deer), explore the House and Formal Gardens, picnic under an ancient tree or take lunch in the Orangery.

Mt Edgumbe's main claim to fame is as a Grade I Historic Garden, one of only 120 in the country, and classed as 'outstanding' by Engish Heritage. Horticulturally it is also outstanding as the holder of the National Camellia Collection – more than 600 species and hybrids thrive here, the responibility of Maggie Campbell-Culver, a garden historian and manager of the whole estate.

The ten acres of Formal Gardens are mostly sheltered by robust Ilex Oak, enabling the growth of exotic flowers and shrubs from all over the world. Thus one can see authentic French, Italian, New Zealand and American Gardens. There is also, of course, an English Garden, with huge Cork Oaks, plus a Fern Dell and Rose Garden. Adjacent to the House is the Earl's Garden, with splendid lawns and many magnificent trees, including a rare Lucombe Oak. Throughout the gardens are superb statues, fountains, temples and follies, ballustrading and a grotto (the 'Shell Seat').

OPEN: All year - Park and Formal Gardens (entry free); March 31st - Oct 31st - House & Earls Garden, from 11am to 5pm Wed - Sun plus Bank Hols. TEAROOM & GIFTSHOPS open daily March - Oct. Facilities for disabled. Dogs allowed in park.

HOMELEIGH GARDEN CENTRE
Dutson, nr Launceston.
Tel: (01566) 773147
Fax: (01566) 773547

Angling is second only to gardening as an outdoor leisure pursuit, and both are well catered for at this 'dual' centre 1½ miles from Launceston on the A388 Holsworthy road.

Derek and Enis Broad, both well known in the area, started the business in 1982 as a nursery, since when it has progressed rapidly to become one of the largest garden centres (member of HTA) in Cornwall. The angling centre, opened in February 1993, features ponds, fountain ornaments, a wide range of tackle and baits and all kinds of accessories. The River Tamar flows not far from here, and fine views over the valley and Dartmoor are to be had from the large tree and shrub area.

Also of special note are the garden furniture (many leading brands are stocked), greenhouses and garden sheds. Paved paths and automatic doors make life very easy for the disabled.

OPEN: 8am to 5pm Mon - Sat; 10:30am to 4:30pm Sundays.

Aquatics/fish	✔	Garden furniture	✔	Ornaments/statues	✔
Bookshop	✔	Greenhouses for sale	✔	Pets/accessories	✔
Car park	✔	Houseplants	✔	Play area	✔
Conservatories	✘	Information desk	✔	Restaurant/cafeteria	✔
Clothing	✔	Landscaping service	✘	Sheds etc	✔
Floristry	✘	Machinery	✘	Swimming pools	✘

GARDEN HOUSE
**Buckland Monachorum, nr Yelverton.
Tel: (01822) 854769**

With over 6,000 different types of plant, this is one of the largest collections in the region. A sterile plant museum it is not, however, representing as it does a triumph of harmony with nature. The garden lies on a north-facing slope nearly 500 ft above sea level and has a very high rainfall of 55"-60" per annum. The natural soil is very acidic, but over the centuries parts of the walled garden have been limed, greatly enhancing the prospects of growing a wide range of plants well.

Started by the Fortescue family in 1945 in the walled garden of a ruined 16th-century vicarage, the gardens have evolved to the marvel one sees today. In particular the two-acre teraced garden is arguably one of the most romantic and beautiful in the entire country. There is also a Rhododendron Walk, Acer Glade, Quarry Garden, Old Cottage Garden, an Herbaceous Glade, Magic Circle, Wild Flower Meadow – indeed, a medley of very different habitats, and with wonderful views over the Devon and Cornwall countryside.

Since the death of Lionel Fortescue in 1981, the gardens have been run by

Keith and Ros Wiley, who continue to develop and expand – eight acres are now cultivated.

Light lunches and scrumptious cream teas are served in the front rooms of the house. There's also a PLANT CENTRE selling a wide selection of helthy specimens.

OPEN: 10:30am to 5pm every day from March 1st to Oct. 31st.

ENDSLEIGH GARDEN CENTRE
Ivybridge.
Tel: (01752) 892254
Fax: (01752) 690284

One of the region's biggest and most frequented garden centres, Endsleigh was established some 20 years ago and occupies no less than eight acres, including 40,000 sq ft under cover. Here you will find a range of specialist operators covering every conceivable requisite. Among them is one of the largest water garden suppliers in the country, a pet shop, a patio department, a mower specialist and even mountain bikes! Garden furniture is a forte - the choice is enormous - and there's also a full quota of garden decor and barbecue equipment. Special mention must be made of the Plantation Tea Shop: no plastic food with seating to match - quality is the watchword, which extends to the local produce for sale (preserves, cakes, biscuits etc).

With all this plus a children's play area, Endsleigh is obviously a great place for a day out with the family, but as a member of the HTA and Garden Centres Association it is also one for the serious gardener. The layout is first rate, and all the plants are clearly identified. As well as a landscaping service, there are four infor-

mation centres dispensing advice on plant selection, nurturing, soil, location etc.

OPEN: daily 9am to 5pm (from 10am Sundays) in winter, 9am (10am Sundays) to 6pm in summer.

Aquatics /fish	✔	Information desk	✔
Bookshop	✔	Landscaping service	✘
Car park	✔	Machinery	✘
Conservatories	✘	Ornaments /statues	✔
Clothing	✔	Pets /accessories	✔
Floristry	✘	Play area	✔
Garden furniture	✔	Restaurant /cafeteria	✔
Greenhouses for sale	✔	Sheds etc	✔
Houseplants	✔	Swimming pools	✘

OTTER NURSERIES (TORBAY) Ltd

250 Babbacombe Road, Torquay.
(approx. 1 mile from Torquay
Harbour, nr Palace Hotel)
Tel: (01803) 214294
Fax: (01803) 291481

Nestled in a sheltered disused quarry (shared with Smith's Do-It-All), this branch of Otter Nurseries was opened in 1984. The long-established sister (or should it be mother?) centre is at Ottery St Mary, where all the plants are grown, delivered daily. Although a smaller site, the car park accommodates 300 vehicles, and the good-sized shop stocks a full range of chemicals and other gardening requisites. The range of plants is also sizeable, as are the seasonal displays of furniture, bulbs and Christmas goods. Of special note is the excellent floristry (run by Fran, wife of manager Keith Powell), affiliated to British Teleflower, which makes daily deliveries of fresh flowers and eye-catching arrangements throughout the Torbay area. Houseplants and garden ornaments are also well represented.

OPEN: 9am to 5:30pm Mon - Sat; 10am to 5pm Sundays.

Aquatics / fish	✗	Information desk	✗
Bookshop	✗	Landscaping service	✗
Car park	✔	Machinery	✗
Conservatories	✗	Ornaments / statues	✔
Clothing	✗	Pets / accessories	✗
Floristry	✔	Play area	✗
Garden furniture	✔	Restaurant / cafeteria	✗
Greenhouses for sale	✗	Sheds etc	✗
Houseplants	✔	Swimming pools	✗

JACK'S PATCH GARDEN CENTRE
Newton Road, Bishopsteignton.
Tel: (01626) 776996

On the shores of the beautiful Teign estuary, the 'Patch' is in fact a very sizeable acreage of nursery and comprehensive garden centre. From humble beginnings 50 years ago, the site has developed into one of the region's best. The business remains family-run, however, by brothers Peter and Jeremy Hepworth.

For all its diversification, the garden centre also remains true to its origins as a plant specialist. The range of plants is enormous, but 85% are home-grown, and a confident 12-month guarantee is offered on all hardy plants. Staff are friendly and knowledgeable garden enthusiasts, and always keen to chat about gardening and share their knowledge.

As well as plants, there is a well stocked gift shop, a children's playpark, a tropical and cold water fish shop and good food at 'Jack's Kitchen.'

OPEN: 9am - 5:30pm Mon. to Sat., 10am - 5:30pm Sun. & Bank Hols. Closes 5pm from Nov. to Feb. inclusive.

Aquatics /fish	✔	Garden furniture	✔	Ornaments /statues	✔
Bookshop	✔	Greenhouses for sale	✔	Pets /accessories	✘
Car park	✔	Houseplants	✔	Play area	✔
Conservatories	✔	Information desk	✔	Restaurant /cafeteria	✔
Clothing	✔	Landscaping service	✘	Sheds etc	✔
Floristry	✘	Machinery	✘	Swimming pools	✘

ST. BRIDGET NURSERIES Ltd
Old Rydon Lane, Exeter.
Tel: (01392) 873672
Fax: (01392) 876710

Very much a grower's nursery, this, as well as a first class general garden centre. You will find a wide selection of unusual plants, and 95% of all the trees, shrubs, roses, bedding plants, herbaceous and seasonal plants are 'home grown' in the nurseries' 100 acres and more, including rose fields which are open to the public from early July. There is also a large propagation unit in which is a micro propagation laboratory.

So there is much to interest the enthusiast, but the more casual gardener will also benefit from a day out here and at the sister branch, just two miles away at CLYST St MARY. Children have a small play area, and you could round the day off with a pie or cream tea in the restaurant. Clyst St Mary also has an aquatic centre. Seasonal flowers are fresh-cut for the floristry.

The business was established in 1925, and is now in the hands of the third generation of the same family. It is a member of the GCA, HTA, and Rose Growers Association.

OPEN: Oct. to March 8am - 5pm Mon to Sat, 9am to 4:30pm Sundays & Bank Hols; March to Oct. 8am - 5:30pm, 9am - 5pm Sundays & Bank Hols.

Aquatics /fish (at Clyst)	✔	Information desk	✔
Bookshop	✔	Landscaping service	✗
Car park	✔	Machinery	✗
Conservatories	✔	Ornaments /statues	✔
Clothing	✗	Pets /accessories	✔
Floristry	✔	Play area	✔
Garden furniture	✔	Restaurant /cafeteria	✔
Greenhouses for sale	✔	Sheds etc	✔
Houseplants	✔	Swimming pools	✗

OTTER NURSERIES Ltd

**Gosford Road, Ottery St Mary, Devon
(approx. 1 mile off A30 – turn at
Pattesons Cross)
Tel: (01404) 815815
Fax: (01404) 815816**

One of the largest garden centres in the country, Otter Nurseries was started by Marilyn and Malcolm White, who are still running the business with the active participation of five of their children and a total staff of 160. Over the years the site has been continually developed, so that there is now a vast area under cover and every facility for a full and enjoyable day out.

The range of plants has few equals anywhere, and the stocks of shrubs, herbaceous plants, conifers and trees are quite exceptional. During the autumn a staggering 40 tonnes plus of Daffodil and Narcissi bulbs alone are in addition to many more unusual ones. Quality is also first rate: virtually all the plants are grown on the 80-acre site. The many awards won bear witness to this, including runner-up in the 'Garden Centre of the Year' competition. Everything you might expect to see in a garden is here, but special mention must be made of furniture: the choice is truly massive. From October until Christmas the furniture department becomes a 'Winter Wonderland' of Christmas decorations. There's also a large display of garden buildings, including conservatories, summerhouses, sheds and many sizes of greenhouses.

The restaurant is worth a visit on its own merit. Always busy, it serves wonderful homecooked food – anything from a snack to a main meal – at very reasonable prices.

*OPEN: 9am - 5:30pm Mon - Sat;
10:30am to 4:30pm Sundays.*

Aquatics/fish	✔	Information desk	✔
Bookshop	✔	Landscaping service	✔
Car park	✔	Machinery	✔
Conservatories	✔	Ornaments/statues	✔
Clothing	✔	Pets/accessories	✘
Floristry	✘	Play area	✘
Garden furniture	✔	Restaurant/cafeteria	✔
Greenhouses for sale	✔	Sheds etc	✔
Houseplants	✔	Swimming pools	✘

SCOTT'S NURSERIES (MERRIOTT) LTD

Higher Street, Merriott.
Tel: (01460) 72306
Fax: (01460) 77433

This is not an easy place to find. From the A303 look for Ilminster town signs (avoid by-pass), then take the Crewkerne road at Lopen Head Roundabout. Scott's is sign-posted to your left as you enter the village. From the A30 turn north onto the A356 in the square in Crewkerne. The road to Merriott is the first on the left about one mile out of town. Continue on this road into the village of Merriott. Scott's is sign-posted on your right almost as you leave the village. If still in doubt, ring the garden centre, as it will be well worth persevering.

Nationally known, Scott's is one of the longest established nurseries in the country – there has been one on this site for over 200 years. A member of the HTA, it stocks just about every known hardy garden plant, and the ranges of fruit trees and roses are amongst the most extensive in Britain, if not the world! The rosefields provide a tapestry of colour and fragrance all through the summer. Happily for those who cannot visit in person there is a MAIL ORDER service for the full range of plants grown, which is detailed in a catalogue.

Those fortunate enough to be able to do so will find much else of interest, and disabled readers will be pleased to know that there are toilet facilities for them.

OPEN: 9am to 5pm, Mon - Sat; 10:30am to 4:30pm Sundays.

Aquatics/fish	✗	Information desk	✔
Bookshop	✔	Landscaping service	✗
Car park	✔	Machinery	✗
Conservatories	✔	Ornaments/statues	✔
Clothing	✔	Pets/accessories	✗
Floristry	✔	Play area	✗
Garden furniture	✔	Restaurant/cafeteria	✔
Greenhouses for sale	✗	Sheds etc	✔
Houseplants	✔	Swimming pools	✗

MONKTON ELM GARDEN CENTRE

West Monkton, Heathfield,
nr Taunton.
Tel: (01823) 412381
Fax: (01823) 412745

The oldest nursery in the Taunton area, Monkton Elm occupies nearly eight acres, and is further unique in having a bandstand, used quite often for concerts. Pleasantly situated just over two miles from Taunton town centre (between the A38 and A361), many customers travel a good distance to what has developed into one of the most comprehensive garden centres in the region, owned entirely by David and Luella Bellman.

Attractively and clearly laid out, the site is a pleasure to stroll around. A full range of plants, shrubs and trees is well signed and labelled, but for more detailed advice the staff are all fully qualified and willing to help. Although not a landscaping service as such, the Garden Design Dept will be pleased to assist you in planning. Under cover are two very large shopping areas, with a full range of goods to numerous to be listed here.

With a restaurant and play area as well, the centre has all one could wish for a good day out with the family, and you may be fortunate enough to catch a concert, too!

OPEN: 9:30am to 5:30 pm every day.

Aquatics/fish	✔	Information desk	✔
Bookshop	✔	Landscaping service	✘
Car park	✔	Machinery	✔
Conservatories	✔	Ornaments/statues	✔
Clothing	✔	Pets/accessories	✔
Floristry	✔	Play area	✔
Garden furniture	✔	Restaurant/cafeteria	✔
Greenhouses for sale	✔	Sheds etc	✔
Houseplants	✔	Swimming pools	✔

HESTERCOMBE HOUSE GARDENS

Cheddon Fitzpaine, nr Taunton.
Tel: (01823) 337222

Those two doyens of country house and garden design, Sir Edwin Lutyens and Gertrude Jekyll, collaborated to create this supreme example of the art. Established in 1904, the garden has been restored in recent years by Somerset County Council, following Jekyll's original planting plans.

Lutyens had to accept the house and upper terrace as they were, but he took full advantage of the sloping ground to form a series of terraces and vistas around a formal sunken plat bounded by a long pergola, through which one can view the lovely surrounding countryside. A rotunda linked this to a narrow terrace to the east of the house on which he sited the Orangery and Dutch Garden. To the west is the Rose Garden, wherein one can observe Jekyll's hallmark, the use of diminishing clay pots sunk inside each other within a French burr millstone. Water ripples through a central rill.

Grey is, as one might expect, the dominant colour of the Grey Walk, but other reinforcing colours are used in drifts, and as always with Jekyll, scent and texture are very important. The East and West Rills are architecturally identical, the raised terraces reminiscent of an Elizabethan garden, but the West is mainly shrubs and roses while the East is mostly yellow/orange herbaceous. In the centre of it all is the plat, a masterpiece of the partnership.

A treat for the eyes between May and July, Hestercombe is about the marriage of geometry with nature, form with colour, further harmonised by the sounds of moving water throughout.

OPEN: 9am to 5pm Mon - Fri all year round, plus 2pm to 5pm Sats & Suns from May to September.

WEST SOMERSET GARDEN CENTRE

Mart Road, Minehead.
Tel: (01643) 703812
Fax: (01643) 706470

Weather information is vital to the keen gardener, and this 14-year-old centre is the first to know – handily, the Met. Office weather station is on the site, and a detailed forecast is issued every morning, along with figures for the previous day's sunshine, rainfall and temperature.

No doubt this information is put to good use in the centre's own growing unit at Dunster, where all the bedding plants and most of the shrubs (a speciality, along with trees) are reared. There is a wide variety of unusual plants, but staff are equal to it and are able to offer sound advice, drawing on solid experience and training.

The well-stocked shop has an indoor plant area, and the 'home-made' theme continues in the cafe, where fresh cakes, scones, filled rolls and sandwiches are served.

The centre, a member of the HTA, fully lives up to its name, and serves the whole of the western limb of the county. Significantly, ever more customers are drawn in from north Devon also. If you are touring the area the centre would prove a worthwhile and pleasant diversion from the normal haunts.

OPEN: 8am to 8pm Mon - Sat, 10am to 4pm Sundays. Note that Sunday opening varies in winter.

Aquatics/fish	✔	Information desk	✔
Bookshop	✔	Landscaping service	✔
Car park	✔	Machinery	✘
Conservatories	✘	Ornaments/statues	✔
Clothing	✘	Pets/accessories	✘
Floristry	✘	Play area	✘
Garden furniture	✔	Restaurant/cafeteria	✔
Greenhouses for sale	✔	Sheds etc	✔
Houseplants	✔	Swimming pools	✘

RODE BIRD GARDENS
Rode, nr Bath.
Tel: (01373) 830326
Fax: (01373) 831288

'Brolly' (pictured) is something of a TV personality, having appeared with Johnny Morris on 'Animal Magic.' He is an especially fortunate Umbrella Cockatoo in living in these lovely gardens, just off the A36 Bath to Warminster road.

Being the most beautiful of all creatures, birds are a natural complement and adornment to any garden. Before the opening of the Tropical Bird Gardens in 1962, the grounds had been sadly neglected. Founders Donald and Betty Risdon began the monumental task of restoring it. 4,000 tons of mud were taken from the lake and ponds, the silt and rubble used to form the base of the modern gardens and flower beds. Dead trees and shrubs were removed and a programme of planting and cultivation was initiated. Over the years thousands of bulbs, shrubs and roses have been planted, always with the aim of presenting the birds in as natural environment as possible. Wild flowers which have become endangered elsewhere flourish at Rode.

But it is the clematis which is queen of the flora here. Mrs Risdon is Membership

Secretary of the British Clematis Society, and now has a collection of 160 in the grounds. Note that there is a special CLEMATIS WEEKEND on 15th and 16th July, 1995. Herbaceous plants are also encouraged, as there is plenty of room for them in which to spread.

There is a cafeteria licensed in summer (light refreshment only in winter). There are a play area for children, facilities for the disabled and information centre. The 7¼" gauge Rode WOODLAND RAILWAY runs from Easter to October.

OPEN: 10am to 6pm daily in summer, 10am to dusk in winter. Last admittance one hour before closing.

BRACKENWOOD GARDEN CENTRE

131 Nore Road, Portishead, nr Bristol.
Tel: (01275) 843484

On a clear day one can see right across the Bristol Channel and up to the Severn Bridge from this lovely hillside site. Noted for its unique character, this family-run centre (member of HTA) has been established over 25 years. From being a hobby for John and Jenny Maycock it has emerged as a plantsman's paradise; within its 10 acres is an enormous range of plants, amongst which trees and shrubs are specialities, some quite rare and many grown in the centre's own nurseries. There's also an exceptional choice of herbaceous plants.

The qualified staff are amiable and helpful, and moving towards biological rather than chemical controls. But the centre has much to offer even those who live in a tower block: a large craft area, for example, a very good range of houseplants and floristry, and delicious home-cooking in the very pleasant tearoom. Plus, of course, the beautiful Woodland Garden (see opposite).

OPEN: 9am to 5:30pm every day except Christmas period.

Aquatics/fish	✔	Information desk	✔
Bookshop	✔	Landscaping service	✘
Car park	✔	Machinery	✘
Conservatories	✘	Ornaments/statues	✔
Clothing	✘	Pets/accessories	✘
Floristry	✔	Play area	✘
Garden furniture	✘	Restaurant/cafeteria	✔
Greenhouses for sale	✘	Sheds etc	✘
Houseplants	✔	Swimming pools	✘

WOODLAND GARDEN AT BRACKENWOOD

**Nore Road, Portishead, nr Bristol.
Tel: (01275) 843484**

Brackenwood's 'secret' garden lies on the hillside behind the garden centre (see opposite); it should not be missed. Its 10 acres of woodland burst into life in spring, the rhododendrons, azaleas, camellias and pieris resplendent in a spectrum of colour on the wooded hillside, aided by Chilean fire trees, magnolias, hydrangeas and witch hazels. Some of our finest native trees vie with an array of introduced species bordering the many grassy paths and the garden's many ponds and pools.

But it's not just the wonderful flora of the garden which have made this an ever-growing attraction, and caused Jarrolds of Norwich to depict it on the front of their Beautiful Gardens of Britain Calendar (1994): there's an abundance of fauna in the form of squirrels, badgers, foxes, woodpeckers and waterfowl, the latter in their own special enclosure.

So whether you are an enthusiast for horticulture or just a simple lover of nature, Brackenwood holds out the prospect of a very stimulating and agreeable day out.

WOODBOROUGH GARDEN CENTRE & NURSERIES

Nursery Farm, Woodborough, nr Pewsey.
Tel: (01672) 851249

The Vale of Pewsey was one of the very first parts of the country to be settled by Man, being of rich soil, mild climate and fed by the River Avon. Yet today it is one of the most sparsely populated areas of southern England, and consequently a delight to live in and to visit. The Romans grew grapes here, but it was in daffodils that founder W.T. Ware made his name, after having started out with roses in 1883. To this day the 300-acre farm grows pick-your-own daffodils, tulips, vegetables and soft fruits. The spectacular fields of shimmering colour draw many visitors in spring.

Much of what is produced on the nursery finds its way to the nearby two-acre, family-run garden centre (member of HTA) and its 1750 sq ft shop. Approx. one quarter of an acre is given over to display gardens, and about the same to a canopy under which a full range of quality, carefully-labelled plants is well presented. Climbers are a speciality, notably Clematis, of which some 100 varieties have been stocked. Some of the more uncommon include armandii Apple Blossom, texensis Etoile Rose and texensis Duchess of Albany. There are also 200 sq ft of houseplants, plus floristry materials, ornaments, Asian, dry stone and terracotta pots, books, dry goods and paving. Mrs Brewin manages the centre, aided by Madge Halsey who has worked here for over 40 years.

Open: 9am to 5pm Mon - Sat; 10am to 4pm Sundays.

Aquatics /fish	✗	Information desk	✗
Bookshop	✓	Landscaping service	✗
Car park	✓	Machinery	✗
Conservatories	✗	Ornaments/statues	✓
Clothing	✗	Pets/accessories	✗
Floristry	✓	Play area	✓
Garden furniture	✓	Restaurant/cafeteria	✓
Greenhouses for sale	✗	Sheds etc	✗
Houseplants	✓	Swimming pools	✗

STOURTON HOUSE FLOWER GARDEN

Stourton, nr Warminster.
Tel: (01747) 840417

Right next to the famous Stourhead Landscape Garden, three miles north-west of Mere by the A303, Stourton's four acres are very much for plant lovers. Having been featured on BBC's 'Gardener's World' and other television programmes, Stourton is itself no stranger to fame.

This is a garden full of ideas and surprises. Grass paths lead the visitor through many varied vistas of colourful shrubs, trees and a host of unusual plants. Hydrangeas are surely the long suit, with no fewer than 250 diferent types best seen in the latter half of summer, but the daffodils are also spectacular in spring. In between there is a continual feast of colour, from the long-established rhododendrons and azaleas, to delphiniums, roses, the intriguingly-named chocolate plant and many more. Stourton has won many prizes at RHS shows.

The pond, home to the incomparable water lilies and overlooked by an arbour, was formed from the cavity left by a huge beech tree which blew down – it is fed by water from the roof of the house. Another smaller and more formal pond with numerous carniverous plants is the centrepiece of the fine herbaceous garden, approached by the lovely '12 Apostles Walk'. A Woodland Garden and Camellia Walk are to be found in the opposite corner, near which is the Secret Garden. Seating has been thoughtfully placed throughout, and wheelchairs are not a problem.

The plant shop sells many uncommon plants and a very wide range of hydrangeas. Dried flowers are another speciality, grown in the garden and beautifully presented. Don't leave without trying the substantial home-made fare served on the flowery verandahs or on the lawn. There's also a pub in the village.

OPEN: 11am to 6pm Easter Sunday to end of November on Weds, Thurs, Suns & Bank Hols. Also special Open Days and Plantsman's Days. Dogs not permitted.

CHIFFCHAFFS GARDEN & ABBEY PLANTS NURSERY
Chaffeymoor, Bourton, nr Gillingham. Tel: (01747) 840841

It is hard to believe that this dream of a cottage garden, so often featured in magazines, books and on television, was virtually a wasteland until 1979. It is of great credit to the private owners, who, taking advantage of the sheltered valley position, skilfully terraced the sloping site, creating a split level garden full of nooks and crannies, and with glimpses of the lovely Blackmoor Vale.

Approached by an avenue of flowering cherries, the 16th-century cottage provides a fine backdrop to the wonderful array of intense colour and form. The soil is acidic, and the range of trees and plants grown is admirable, with spring bulbs, camellias, flowering shrubs, herbaceous and shrub roses planted informally in beds separated by curving lawns, giving the garden a very long season of interest.

An attractive short walk between beds of bluebells and wild flowers brings you to the woodland garden laced with streams, where acid-loving rhododendrons and azaleas put on a spectacular show, whilst beneath their canopy primula, gunnera and rheums thrive in the moist conditions.

Photo: John Glover

Adjacent to the garden is a good small nursery, selling an excellent range of healthy plants at very reasonable prices. There is no mail order service. Home-made teas are available on the last Sunday of each month, on Bank Holiday weekends and by prior arrangement for groups.

OPEN: garden from March 26th to Sept. 24th, Weds, Thurs & Suns, 2pm to 5pm; closed 2nd Sunday of each month. Admission fee £1.50 in aid of NGS. NURSERY: all year Tues to Sat (plus garden open times), 10am to 1pm, 2pm to 5pm.

CHETTLE HOUSE
Chettle, nr Blandford
Tel: (01258) 830209
Fax: (01258) 830380

'Chettle' derives from the old English word for a deep valley (the word 'kettle' is a relation), and these rolling chalklands have been cultivated since before the dawn of written history.

The house (open to the public) is a fine example of the Queen Anne period in the English Baroque style by Thomas Archer – he favoured rounded corners. Custodians of this long history are current owners Patrick and Janet Bourke, who have worked hard to bring the house to its present high standard – beautifully preserved and well furnished in the fashion of that age. Part of it is given over to an art gallery.

Wide lawns frame the house, and in the five acres of grounds grow many chalk-loving shrubs and outstanding herbaceous plants, some rare. The effect is very pleasant and relaxing.

Plants raised in the garden are sold in the small NURSERY, not far from the house. Light refreshments are also available.

OPEN: 11am to 5pm daily except Tuesdays and Saturdays, from Good Friday until the second Sunday in October. The house stands six miles north-east of Blandford off the A354.

Nets! Nets! Nets!

Fruit cages
The only effective protection of soft fruit from birds.

We also supply:

Plant support netting for herbaceous borders

Garden Netting

Tennis Nets

Grass Court Surrounds

Price list from:

KNOWLE NETS (dept GS)
East Road, Bridport,
Dorset DT6 4NX
Tel: (01308) 424342

KNOWLE nets

ABBOTSBURY SUB-TROPICAL GARDENS
Abbotsbury, nr Weymouth.
Tel: (01305) 871387

"But the glory of the Garden lies in more than meets the eye" – Kipling. The author's observation is nowhere more apposite than here at Abbotsbury.

The story begins in 1765, when the first countess of Ilchester built Abbotsbury Castle on a bluff overlooking Chesil Beach. That castle is now a ruin, but the garden has continued to develop, acquiring over the years many rare and exotic plants. Of particular note is a grove of ancient Camellias which are probably from the original introduction in 1792 from Japan. There are also two specimens of the rare Piccomia excelsa and a large Podocarpus.

Many of the trees and plants have been flourishing here for well over 100 years, although native to much warmer climes. The secret lies in the location: this part of the south coast enjoys more sunshine than anywhere else on the mainland, and a moderate rainfall. This helps to ripen the wood of many plants, thereby rendering them hardier than those grown in wetter areas. Other factors are the low hills which protect the site from cold northerlies, a blanketing tree canopy and the proximity to that giant radiator, the sea. In short, here is a beneficent micro-climate.

First port of call will probably be the walled garden; here you will find tearooms, a sunken garden and the original Victorian Garden with its huge Chusan Palms, among the tallest in Britain.

The gardens are divided in two by a stream which forms three ponds. There are many routes around the gardens, and so much to see. Exit from the Victorian Garden and you will come across a row of cannons salvaged from the Spanish Armada. Behind them is a conservatory housing plants too tender even for Abbotsbury. Turn and walk through the new Winter Garden, then right into the Secret Walk, planted with rare Chinese plants, which leads into the Himalayan Glade. Crossing the bridge will lead you to Hydrangea Walk and Azalea Path. Heading back now a right turn up Long Walk past shrub roses (with herbaceous border to your right) takes you to the New Zealand Border and formal lily ponds.

You will have earned your cup of tea while the children romp in the play area. On the way out, don't miss the South American border, PLANT CENTRE & SHOP. You will still not have seen everything, but there's always another day!

OPEN: Summer daily 10am - 5pm (last admission); Winter - please ring for details. Abbotsbury is on the B3157 between Weymouth and Bridport. The village itself, full of arts and crafts, is well worth a browse.

HUMPHRIES GARDEN CENTRE & WILDLIFE GARDEN
Littlemoor Road, Weymouth.
Tel: (01305) 834766
Fax: (01305) 832708

Situated in a lush green valley with the gentle climate of the Dorset coast, Humphries (HTA) occupies an ideal site for a centre "dedicated to the total garden experience". And indeed almost every conceivable garden need can be met here, with some useful 'extras' too.

A key stockist for the famous Blooms of Bressingham, the highly regarded plantaria is noted for quality and presentation. Friendly and informative staff are always on hand to dispense advice to both amateur and experienced gardener. The garden shop is treasure store of all kinds of accessories, barbecues, ceramics and, in season, exciting Christmas fare. If that were not enough, there's also a FARM SHOP plus "AARDVARK'S POTTERY".

Saunter round the quality garden buildings and conservatories without pressure but always with expert advice to call on. After a good meal or just a cake in the restaurant, don't forget to visit the beautiful wildlife garden, run by the Dorset Trust for Nature Conservation.

Aquatics /fish	✔	Information desk	✔
Bookshop	✔	Landscaping service	✔
Car park	✔	Machinery	✗
Conservatories	✔	Ornaments /statues	✔
Clothing	✔	Pets /accessories	✔
Floristry	✔	Play area	✔
Garden furniture	✔	Restaurant/cafeteria	✔
Greenhouses for sale	✔	Sheds etc	✔
Houseplants	✔	Swimming pools	✔

OPEN: 9am to 5pm Mon - Fri; 9am to 6pm Sat; 10:30am to 4:30pm Sun.

STEWARTS COUNTRY GARDEN CENTRE

God's Blessing Lane, Broomhill, Holt, nr Wimborne.
Tel: (01202) 882462
Fax: (01202) 842127

Widely acknowledged as opening Britain's "first" garden centre (in 1953), Stewarts (H.T.A., G.C.A.) have remained at the forefront of the trade, both here and at the other site at Somerford, near Christchurch.

There could hardly be a more idyllic setting for a garden centre, but there's much more than that to bring you to this quiet, aptly named country lane. Don't miss the animals (including Vietnamese pot-bellied pigs) and do walk the Nursery Trail, which includes Jim's Pond, a butterfly garden, native plant collection and birch collection. Between June and September on Mondays, Wednesdays and Fridays tours of the nursery are organised (no charge), an opportunity to see where and how the plants for the centre are grown.

The plants are of a high standard and beautifully presented, mostly on raised benches. There's a particularly good display of greenhouses for sale. The bookshop and floristry are first rate, and you could also pick up china, houseplants or homemade sweets and honey – all very suitable as gifts. Naturally, in the large shop you will find a full range of gardening goods and barbecues. Staff are well informed and amiable. The restaurant is very agreeable and good value.

OPEN: 9am to 6pm Mon - sat; 11am to 5pm Sundays.

Aquatics / fish	✔	Information desk	✔
Bookshop	✔	Landscaping service	✘
Car park	✔	Machinery	✘
Conservatories	✔	Ornaments / statues	✔
Clothing	✔	Pets / accessories	✔
Floristry	✔	Play area	✔
Garden furniture	✔	Restaurant / cafeteria	✔
Greenhouses for sale	✔	Sheds etc	✔
Houseplants	✔	Swimming pools	✘

KNOLL GARDENS
Hampreston, nr Wimborne.
Tel: (01202) 873931
Fax: (01202) 870842

Viewers of Gardeners' World and That's Gardening will have seen these award-winning gardens before, but television cannot compare to a visit 'in the flesh.' Beautifully landscaped, they are filled with water gardens, ponds, waterfalls, streams, rockeries, herbaceous borders, woodland glens, colourful formal areas, original sculptures and much more; a striking example of what can be done with just six acres, and features are changed annually.

Each season has its own delights: the dazzling hues of the magnificent rhodo-dendrons and azaleas in spring, as well as spring bulbs, followed by the spectacle and form of the herbaceous borders and bedding plants, the gorgeous display wall of fuchsias on the approach drive, and finally the bronzes of the many trees in wistful autumn. Planting is on an intimate scale, and many rare and exotics species are among the 4,000 named (labelling is very helpful). Smooth paths, lawns and strategically placed seating enables the elderly and infirm to also derive maximum pleasure.

Having refreshed the spirit, temporal needs are taken care of at the Visitors' Centre, where there's a good licensed restaurant with fine views on the first floor, and a tearoom at ground level – cream teas for groups can be arranged at

set times, and coach parties are welcome. Browse through the large plant sales area, gifts and bookshop, and you may be interested in the 8-minute video detailing the history of Knoll Gardens (RHS, HTA, once known as Wimborne Botanic Garden) over the past 25 years. New owners Neil Lucas and John and Janet Flude have exciting plans for the future.

OPEN: 10am to 5:30pm daily, 1st March to 1st November. Group visits by arrangement on summer evenings and in winter.

JAMES TREHANE & SONS Ltd, CAMELLIA NURSERY

Stapehill Road,
Hampreston, nr Wimborne.
Tel & Fax: (01202) 873490

"But we had no idea it would be so large and so interesting." That is a fairly typical remark from an amazed first-time visitor to this very special, family-run nursery. Under a quarter-of-an-acre of glass and in about three acres of sheltered outdoor area grows a glorious array of magnificent Camellias, approx. 350 varieties ranging in size up to the very large "instant garden" specimens, all in containers.

The business was founded in 1959 by David Trehane (son of farmer James Trehane), aided by daughter Jennifer. It was established around a natural spring which he had found in sheltered woodland, and which has a pH of 4.8 – very acidic and ideal for Camellias. Even through the droughts the spring has continued to bubble, as do the Trehanes! Their enthusiasm and eagerness to assist both the beginner and the knowledgeable is shared by the staff, and is doubtlessly the cornerstone of their success. They are internationally acknowledged as leading experts on these most regal of shrubs, and are very influential in exhibitions, compe-titions, committees and indeed anything at all to do with their cultivation. David (now in his 80's) has written 'Plantsman's Guide to Camellias' and the RHS Wisley Handbook on Camellias. Jennifer has been primarily responsible for the International Camellia Society's booklet 'Camellias – a Basic Guide'.

Whether you are seeking a special plant for a special occasion, something for a small town garden or for a huge estate in Scotland, or even for export, you will not find a better choice nor more expert guidance. Small plants and orders may be sent by mail order, larger consignments by special next day delivery, but a visit in person will be a rewarding experience. You will also find other compatible plants: Azaleas, Rhododendrons, Pieris, Magnolias and the famous North American Highbush Blueberries (attractive fruit-bearing tub plants).

OPEN: 9am to 4pm Mon - Fri, 10am to 4:30pm Sat & Sun from mid-Feb to end of Oct. Closed 23rd Dec. to 4th Jan.

STEWARTS GARDEN-LANDS
**Lyndhurst Road,
Somerford, nr Christchurch.
Tel: (01425) 272244
Fax: (01425) 279723**

One must reach for the superlatives to describe this extensive complex, one of a duo with Stewarts Country Garden Centre, Broomhill, near Wimborne. A car park for 200, plus an overflow for the same number, suggests that gardeners like what they find. The 11-acre site is attractively landscaped, the 30,000 sq ft shop is airy, tidy and colourful, and throughout great attention has been paid to detail.

There's a full range of healthy-looking plants, from herbs to forest trees, many grown in Stewart's own 50-acre nursery. Most are displayed on raised benches, and the clear labelling is enhanced by useful information boards. Staff, too, are most informative, polite and enthusiastic.

Every conceivable product and service is here, some franchised. Add to this an excellent bookshop, 3,000 sq ft of furniture, pottery and gifts, barbecues, homemade sweets and honey, and you see why the large car park is a necessity. Make a day out with the family; the 2,000 sq ft restaurant is pleasant and good value, there's a play area and next door a Sainsbury's!

Aquatics /fish	✔	Information desk	✔
Bookshop	✔	Landscaping service	✔
Car park	✔	Machinery	✔
Conservatories	✔	Ornaments /statues	✔
Clothing	✔	Pets /accessories	✔
Floristry	✔	Play area	✔
Garden furniture	✔	Restaurant /cafeteria	✔
Greenhouses for sale	✔	Sheds etc	✔
Houseplants	✔	Swimming pools	✔

OPEN: 9am to 6pm Mon - Sat; 11am to 5pm Sundays.

EXBURY GARDENS
Exbury, nr Southampton.
Tel: (01703) 891203

Amongst the most glorious woodland gardens in the world, Exbury is a heady celebration of spring, set in a tranquil corner of the New Forest. Its 200 acres by the Beaulieu River are renowned for the spellbinding displays of rhododendrons, azaleas, camellias and magnolias, created and developed by the Rothschild family since the 1920's.

But a visit at other times of the year will also prove most rewarding. Even before the main event, the Winter Garden shows off its early-flowering rarities, and the 10,000- bulb splendour of Daffodil Meadow is a colourful overture to the new season. The Rose Garden is a picture in June, with an encore in September, while the amazing Rock Garden, one of the largest in Europe, is a continually intriguing canvas of texture and colour. The mantle of autumn brings its own special atmosphere to the gardens, the waterside maples being particularly evocative. This is a time for romantic, secluded walks; the River Walk affords fine views over the estuary.

Lunches and cream teas are served in the licensed tearooms, and there is a GIFT SHOP. A wide selection of home-grown rhododendrons and azaleas, and other plants, are available at the PLANT CENTRE.

OPEN: 10am to 5:30pm (or dusk if earlier) daily from 18th Feb to 29th Oct. Note that from July to September opening is confined to the 53 acres of Yard Wood, and a free guide describes the new Summer Trail. Wheelchair access. Coach enquiries welcome.

HAMBROOKS GARDEN CENTRE

135 Southampton Road,
Titchfield, nr Fareham.
(opp. Super Stores on A27)
Tel: (01489) 572285
Fax: (01489) 579470

Although not the largest in the area, this is a delightful garden centre with an outstanding array of plants, shrubs and trees throughout the year. In addition to approx. 2,000 varieties of plants, mainly supplied from the centre's own nurseries, is a very wide selection of landscaping and garden accessories. Hambrooks can also boast a quite unique attraction: six Show Gardens, designed to promote their design and landscaping skills. Each is about the size of a normal rear garden, and each carries its own theme – Cottage Garden, Italian Garden, Woodland, for example. All contain a wealth of ideas for the experienced and not-so-experienced gardener.

With knowledgeable and friendly staff, top quality plants and accessories at competitve prices, Hambrooks is a fine example of what a good garden centre should be, and is conveniently situated not far from the M27.

OPEN: 9am to 5pm daily, except Christmas.

Aquatics	✘	Information desk	✔
Bookshop	✔	Landscaping service	✔
Car park	✔	Machinery	✘
Conservatories	✘	Ornaments/statues	✔
Clothing	✘	Pets/accessories	✘
Floristry	✔	Play area	✘
Garden furniture	✔	Restaurant/cafeteria	✘
Greenhouses for sale	✔	Sheds etc	✔
Houseplants	✔	Swimming pools	✘

GILBERT WHITE'S HOUSE & GARDEN

The Wakes, High Street, Selborne, nr Alton.
Tel: (01420) 511275

This charming village, set amidst beautiful countryside, was home to one of the 18th century's most famous naturalists and gardeners, author of 'The Natural History of Selborne.'

Gilbert White was a gardener all his life, and kept a 'Garden Kalendar' of his work, from which developed the Naturalist's Journal. Thus we can trace the progress of the garden and the delight which he took in it. He grew many new flowers and experimented with rare new vegetables like potatoes and melons (his speciality). Despite modest means, he indulged in garden design, creating in microcosm the great landscape gardens of his contemporaries such as Capability Brown.

Armed with all this documentation, the Trustees have begun to restore the garden and parkland as they were when White lived at Wakes. The plan is due for completion in 1996, but there is much of interest to see today. White's ha-ha still separates garden from park (a new one is also planned),

part of his fruit wall still remains as does his brick path from house to park. The 18th-century orchard has been re-planted and a quincunx (five cypress trees in domino pattern) has been restored to the highest point of the garden. The charming rose garden will incorporate a full range of 18th-century plants grown by White, there is a topiary, attractive sunny herb garden, pond garden which will later become a naturalist's garden, and a well stocked,

unusual plant stand. And then there are the fine views across the garden to beech-clad Selborne Hanger!

The house is included in the modest admission price, and there's the bonus of the OATES MUSEUM, commemorating the great man who walked out into the snow on Scott's Antarctic Expedition. There's also a GIFTSHOP, with an excellent range of gifts and books. Just along the road are two pubs and a licensed restaurant/ tearoom.

OPEN: 11am to 5pm daily from end of March to end of October; weekends only in winter. Snowdrop day in Jan/Feb. Unusual Plants Fair 24/25th June. GROUP VISITS day & evening all year by appointment.

APULDRAM ROSES
Apuldram Lane, Dell Quay,
Chichester.
Tel: (01243) 785769
Fax: (01243) 536973

The rose retains a special place in the affections of most gardeners, and this family-run business, started in 1982, is one of the South's leading exponents (member of HTA, BARB, BRGA, RHS, HEA), selling some 50,000 each year. Not only does it sell roses, they are displayed in a beautiful garden, formerly an orchard, and in a rose field alongside Chichester harbour, a rich tapestry of colour and perfume from June to September. Altogether, around 300 varieties are cultivated, from the old favourites to the very latest introductions.

But if they are to flourish, roses do require care and attention. To help you with this, pruning demonstrations take place daily during the second week of March (you are invited to ask questions), and an Information Room has been added recently. This is next to the shop which sells books, posters, a range of garden ware, ornaments and gifts, plus all that is needed for the care and treatment of roses.

Bare-root roses are available from November to February and can be sent by post anywhere in the UK. Containerised plants are on sale from March to October. A catalogue is produced and can be ordered by post. Orders for the new season's roses may be placed from June 1st.

Group tours may be arranged, and there are Open Evenings in the latter part of June, which involve a guided tour of the rose fields followed by light refreshments in the garden.

OPEN: 9am to 5pm Mon - Sat; 10:30am to 4:30pm Sundays & Bank Hols.

SNOWHILL PLANT & GARDEN CENTRE

**Snowhill Lane,
Copthorne, nr Crawley.
Tel: (01342) 712545
Fax: (01342) 716477**

Snowhill has grown rapidly from humble beginnings, keeping apace with the modern trend. Yet it has never lost sight of its central aims: to offer an extensive range of quality plants and high levels of customer service.

Specialities are conifers, shrubs, roses (including English shrub roses), soft and tree fruit, of which there are large and comprehensive ranges. There's also a very good selection of seasonal perennials and four major seed companies are represented. Indeed, depth of choice and product information are watchwords here; staff are as knowledgable as they are willing to share this knowledge. This is true also of dry goods and garden accessories, which include bird tables and wild bird food, tools, propagators, frames, paving, fencing, peats, composts and landscaping materials. Particularly good is the sizeable range of garden and conservatory furniture. An extensive menu is also available at the fully licensed Planters Coffee Shop, which offers morning coffee, lunch from the carvery and afternoon teas.

The centre is a member of the Tourist Board – another indication of the way the modern trade has developed – as well as the GCA and HTA.

*OPEN: 9am to 6pm
(5:30 in winter) Mon - Sat;
10:30am to 4:30pm
Sundays.*

Aquatics /fish	✔	Information desk	✔
Bookshop	✔	Landscaping service	✔
Car park	✔	Machinery	✔
Conservatories	✘	Ornaments /statues	✔
Clothing	✔	Pets /accessories	✘
Floristry (silk)	✔	Play area	✘
Garden furniture	✔	Restaurant	✔
Greenhouses for sale	✘	Sheds etc	✘
Houseplants	✔	Swimming pools	✘

LEONARDSLEE GARDENS
Lower Beeding, nr Horsham.
Tel: (01403) 891212

Without doubt, these are amongst the finest gardens in the world. Laid out by Sir Edmund Loder from 1889, the 240 acres in a sheltered valley present at every turn a new vision of paradise to catch the breath.

Magnolias, camellias and carpets of daffodils herald the spring, yielding to the spectacular rhododendrons, fragrant azaleas and carpets of bluebells. Of special note is Rhododendron Loderi, raised by Sir Edmund in 1900, covered in enormous pink or white blooms and giving off a luscious perfume. At this time the Rock Garden is also a riot of colour, and many a roll of film has been consumed on this alone. Leave some shots for the marvellous lakeside azaleas, the reflection doubling the effect – there are no less than seven beautiful lakes at Leonardslee, with attendant wildfowl.

As May gives way to June it is the turn of the Kalmias, Oriental Dogwoods and other flowering trees and shrubs. A Summer Wildflower Walk is a new feature, where native species flourish in the absence of chemicals.

Autumn can be as lovely as spring, with the varying hues of the Maples, Hickories, Tupelos and deciduous azaleas.

Other attractions include a BONSAI EXHIBITION and ALPINE GREENHOUSE with over 400 different plants. You may also catch a glimpse of the maintenance crew: there have been WALLABIES in Leonardslee for over 100 years, and they live peacably with the various herds of deer in the grounds. The CLOCK TOWER RESTAURANT and GARDEN CAFE provide a choice of home-made refreshments. The GIFT SHOP has an interesting selection and a wide choice of plants is for sale at the Temperate Greenhouse beside the car park.

OPEN: 10am to 6pm (8pm in May) daily from 1st April to 31st October.

BORDE HILL GARDEN
Haywards Heath (1 1/2 miles north).
Tel: (01444) 450326
Fax: (01444) 440427

"The best kept secret in Sussex" deserves to be better known, for it is a unique collection and truly magical in spring, especially. Surrounded by parkland in an area of outstanding natural beauty, Borde Hill was purchased by Col. Stephenson Clarke in 1893 and has remained in the family up to the present. The colonel sponsored some of the fearless plant hunters of that time, and their legacy is in the many prize-winning blooms at the RHS shows. The most important contribution has been Camellia 'Donation,' introduced in 1941.

Spring is perhaps the best time to visit: the famous magnolias, camellias and rhododendrons (some of them colossal) burst into a blaze of colour, and the woods are carpeted in blubells and thousands of bulbs. A little later the Azalea Ring is a spectacular sight.

The herbaceous border comes into its own in summer, and the Bride's Pool (named after the nearby statue by Antonio Tantardini) is also at its best. For a taste of the sub-tropics don't miss the Round Dell with its exotic palms and bog-loving plants.

The autumn colours paint a marvellous vista in garden and parkland, and the latter remains open all through winter.

There's much more to Borde Hill even than this: special features include a children's adventure playground and holiday activities, tearooms and picnic area, PUB & RESTAURANT, lakeside and woodland walks, PLANT CENTRE & GIFTSHOP, coarse and children's trout fishing, Nerine collection in bloom Sept/Oct, guided tours, outside talks by head gardener, conference and function rooms (ideal for wedding reception). There's also a calendar of special events, eg horse trials, open air theatre, firework and laser symphony, rallies, shows etc.

OPEN: 10am to 6pm daily from 18th March to 1st Oct. Parkland open all year. Wheelchair access. Dogs welcome on leads.

NYMANS GARDEN
Handcross, nr Haywards Heath.
Tel: (01444) 400321

It is quite extraordinary that in the 100 years since Nymans (a plantsman's haven) was created by the Messel family there have been just three head gardeners: James Comber from 1895 to 1953, succeeded by Cecil Nice (who had worked here since 1924) until 1980, then by the current incumbent, David Masters. This unique continuity is surely a factor in the garden's international renown.

But two great disasters have struck during this century: in 1947 the house was virtually destroyed by fire – the ruins, wreathed in climbers, are now a romantic backdrop; worse still, the notorious storm of October 1987 felled 80% of the mature trees, including many rare species. A huge programme of restoration has been a complete success, and today the garden is as charming and peaceful as ever.

The garden is a very large one, but manages to remain essentially intimate and full of surprises. At its heart is the Wall Garden, with much of interest whatever the season. Around the perimeter is a collection of South American plants, many grown from seeds sent over in the 1920's. The Rose Garden is planted with 147 varieties of old-fashioned roses, for which Nymans is famous. The Rock and Heather Garden was one of the first of its kind to be laid out in England, although it is now dominated by pieris, berberis and rhododendrons. The latter, along with azaleas, form a bank of colour in the Tea Garden, where the TEA HOUSE is to be found. A handsome Italian loggia stands in the Sunk Garden, and there also formal lawns, tree walks and a wisteria-clad pergola. A 'wild' meadow is enclosed in the pinetum.

The gardens are owned by the National Trust, there is a SHOP & RESTAURANT in the grounds and extensive plant-sales area.

OPEN: 11am to 6pm (7pm Sat & Sun) or sunset if earlier, Wed - Sun plus Bank Hols, from March to end Oct. Last admissions one hour before closing.

GARDEN PRIDE GARDEN & LEISURE CENTRE

Common Lane, Ditchling.
Tel: (01273) 846844
Fax: (01273) 845540

The great storm of October 1987 inflicted incalculable damage on southern England, but it's an ill wind that blows nobody any good, and out of the ruins of an old nursery destroyed that night arose this first-rate, independent, purpose-built garden centre (member of HTA). Just a quarter-mile north of Ditchling village, one of the county's most picturesque, near to Ditchling Beacon, the highest point in Sussex, and not far from Nymans Garden, it is well placed to offer the prospect of a very complete and satisfying day out.

For an extra special day time your visit for one of the periodic Craft Fairs or Flower Shows (eg orchids, chrysanthemums) – ask for details. There's much else of everyday interest: good selections of silk and dried flowers, clothing, garden furniture, preserves and even cuddly toys! An excellent all-year-round range of gifts and ceramics is augmented by a spectacular Christmas display. A rather nice coffee shop serves home-cooked meals and cakes.

But it is, after all, the plants which make or break a garden centre, and pride is taken in the variety and quality of both indoor and outdoor, the commonplace and the unusual. Although there's no information desk as such, staff are approachable and helpful, the atmosphere always unruffled.

OPEN: 9am to 6pm Mon - Sat (coffee shop 10am to 5pm); 10:30am to 4:30pm Sundays.

Aquatics / fish	✗	Information desk	✗
Bookshop	✔	Landscaping service	✗
Car park	✔	Machinery	✗
Conservatories	✗	Ornaments / statues	✔
Clothing	✔	Pets / accessories	✔
Floristry	✗	Play area	✔
Garden furniture	✔	Restaurant / cafeteria	✔
Greenhouses for sale	✗	Sheds etc	✗
Houseplants	✔	Swimming pools	✗

NOTCUTTS GARDEN CENTRE
**Tonbridge Road, Pembury,
nr Tunbridge Wells.
Tel: (01892) 822636**

One quite forgets that the busy A21 runs right past this attractively laid out centre, one of the smaller of the Notcutts Group but nevertheless fully living up to its high standards.

The stroll from the upper car park, down a park-like landscaped slope, sets the mood. The centrepiece of the planteria is a fountain and pond, out of which runs a little stream crossed by an ornamental bridge. Plants are exceptionally well labelled and sectioned, eg Woodland Plants, Grasses, Ferns. Special Promotions and Patio Section – a forte of Notcutts – are also very good. Hanging baskets are planted up free. All plants are guaranteed for one year provided they have been cared for properly. The choice of ornaments and statues is well above norm.

Inside, garden furniture is strongly represented, there is a small shop selling candles and perfumes, and a display of Arden animal sculptures. Garden machinery is quite limited at present, and clothing restricted to quality boots. There is no cafeteria, although tea and coffee are served at weekends in summer, but there is a large picnic area on a sunny patch at the far side.

OPEN: 8:30am to 5:30pm (5pm in winter, 6pm in spring) Mon - Fri; 9am to 5:30pm (5pm in winter) Saturdays; 11am to 5pm Sundays.

Aquatics	✔	Information desk	✔
Bookshop	✔	Landscaping service	✔
Car park	✔	Machinery	✔
Conservatories	✘	Ornaments/statues	✔
Clothing	✘	Pets/accessories	✘
Floristry	✔	Play area	✔
Garden furniture	✔	Restaurant/cafeteria	✘
Greenhouses for sale	✘	Sheds etc	✘
Houseplants	✔	Swimming pools	✔

WORLD OF WATER
**Hastings Road, Rolvenden,
nr Tenterden.
Tel: (01580) 241771**

Just a mile or so south of Rolvenden on the main road, in one of the prettiest parts of the South East, lies a Mecca for all water gardeners, or indeed anyone who shares in the appreciation of the soothing balm of clear, running water.

To the front is a still lily-pond, crossed by an ornamental bridge, and by the entrance is seating and a fountain or two. But it is behind the building where the true magic is to be found: in less than one acre are countless ponds, of all shapes, sizes and types, each in its own separate garden setting so that one can readily assess how it would look in one's own garden. Some are quite still, others vigorously oxygenated; some are regular and formal, others very natural-looking. Many have a theme: a terrapin pond, for example, a lily pond, a rock garden cascade and many more.

At the centre of the gardens is a lovely pergola feature, dressed in an array of colourful hanging baskets. Indeed, careful attention is paid to all the planting, to get the very best out of the water features, which also encourages beautifully

irridescent damselflies and dragonflies, frogs and the rare great crested newt, almost commonplace here.

The large showroom stocks every conceivable accessory, from plastic ducks to sophisticated filter systems which guarantee green water a thing of the past. Browse amongst the huge aquatic plants section, or marvel at the enormous koi. The aquarium section has 200 tanks of tropical fish. The self-contained water

features could be ideal for your conservatory. Friendly staff offer expert advice and wll gladly answer any queries. World of Water is Europe's biggest water gardening chain, and so can offer a large range at the lowest prices.

There is a cafe by the entrance and ample parking.

OPEN: 9am to 5pm Mon - Sat; 10:30am to 4:30pm Sundays.

PORT LYMPNE MANSION & GARDENS

Port Lympne Estate, Lympne, nr Hythe (exit 11 off M20).
Tel: (01303) 264647
Fax: (01303) 264944

OPEN: 10am to 5pm (3:30pm in winter) every day except Christmas Day.

Port Lympne Mansion, with its 15 acres of terraced gardens, encompasses the essence of the Roman Villas and the English Country House. Overlooking Romney Marsh and the English Channel, Port Lympne is home to over 500 rare and endangered animals accommodated in 300 acres of natural parkland.

The mansion was built for Sir Philip Sassoon between 1911 and 1915, and has been described as 'the last historic house to be built this century'. Its most interesting features are the Moorish Patio, the Rex Whistler Tent Room, an intriguing mosaic floor and the Spencer Roberts Animal Mural Room.

Bought and restored by John Aspinall in 1973, the mansion and gardens have a quiet, unhurried and informal atmosphere. The gardens feature the Clock or Sundial Garden, the Chess Board Garden, Striped garden and Long Border, which runs from the top to the bottom of the garden – 135 yards in all. There is also a small vineyard and figyard. The outer parts of the garden are allowed to grow wild to encourage indigenous wildlife.

Port Lympne has a licensed restaurant and bar, and is available for functions. It also has a giftshop and art gallery. Discounts for groups.

BYBROOK BARN GARDEN CENTRE

Canterbury Road, Kennington,
nr Ashford.
Tel: (01233) 681959
Fax: (01233) 635642

Even in the depths of winter, this enormous shopping complex, just off junction 9 of the M20, has much to tempt one to take the family for a day out. Purpose-built, the covered area alone is over one acre! Yet it all began humbly enough back in 1975 as a mowing machine sales and garden retail outlet, housed in an old barn on the opposite side of the road.

Of course Bybrook is still first and foremost for the gardener, and has a vast range of plants, shrubs and trees, and indeed every garden requisite, amongst which is a particularly huge choice of mowers and other machinery. But there is a veritable Aladdin's Cave of diverse alternatives: a model shop specialising in radio-controlled vehicles and model railways; a carpet, oriental rug and curtains shop; various styles of furniture, including speciality pine; glassware and exotic ornaments; bathrooms and kitchens; wall coverings; an unusual Bonsai shop, with trees ranging in height from nine to 36" and in age from one to 78 years; a pet shop and aquarium, selling tropical fish, exotic birds and fluffy animals – a delight for children, as is the one-acre lake with its abundant wildlife. The Lakeside Cafeteria provides refreshment, cooked lunches, icecreams and a quiet corner to rest the feet awhile.

If you still have the energy, Howletts Wildlife Park, lovely Port Lympne and Leeds Castle are all within easy reach.

OPEN: 9am to 5:30pm Mon - Sat; 10:30am to 4:30pm Sundays.

Aquatics / fish	✔	Information desk	✔
Bookshop	✔	Landscaping service	✗
Car park	✔	Machinery	✔
Conservatories	✔	Ornaments / statues	✔
Clothing	✔	Pets / accessories	✔
Floristry	✔	Play area	✗
Garden furniture	✔	Restaurant / cafeteria	✔
Greenhouses for sale	✔	Sheds etc	✔
Houseplants	✔	Swimming pools	✔

IDEN CROFT HERBS

Frittenden Road, Staplehurst.
Tel: (01580) 891432
Fax: (01580) 892416

Herbs are in the family genes: owner Rosemary (with husband David) Titterington is descended from a lineage all with herbal names. So it was fated that when they bought 12 acres of what was an almost derelict nursery just south of Staplehurst back in 1970, they should develop it into a herb centre and gardens. At first they supplied fresh herbs to industry, caterers, Marks and Spencer and such like, but over the years this has become a centre for tourists and education as well.

Designed to flow into each other, the gardens demonstrate how herbs and aromatic plants can be used for ground cover, colour, scent, therapeutic and decorative purposes throughout the year. They can be seen in all stages of growth and are well labelled and arranged for maximum appreciation – as is the generous seating, placed in sun and shade. The garden holds the National Collection of Mint and Oreganum. The elderly and infirm are well cared for here, and there's even a special garden for the disabled. A lengthy programme of refurbishment is transforming the 17th-century walled

garden, generating an atmosphere of 'natural aromatherapy.' Behind this is a Woodland Walk manned by gnomes. There's also a grassed picnic area.

A full calendar of events, courses and walks is available on request, and the Information Centre is also useful. Naturally there's a shop selling herbs and umpteen related products, and home-made refreshments include herb teas.

OPEN: 9am to 5pm Mon - Sat all year, plus Suns & Bank Hols from March 1st to Sept. 30th. No charge for admission but donations requested so that hospices etc may benefit free. Members of Inst. of Horticulture, British Herb Trades Asscn, HTA. Mail order service.

NOTCUTTS GARDEN CENTRE

Newnham Court, Bearsted Road,
Maidstone.
Tel: (01622) 739944
Fax: (01622) 735887

Just off junction 7 of the M20, this vast site draws custom from many miles around. Established in 1983, one of the very largest garden centres in Kent, it is part of a privately owned group with almost 100 years of experience behind it. The majority of the hardy stock is produced at the company's own nurseries; Notcutt's reputation is built on the quality of the plants, which you will find in abundance in the planteria, carefully presented and labelled. There are also huge displays of ornaments, paving, garden buildings (franchised) etc, and amongst the latter is a novelty mock-Tudor shed with instant child-appeal. Indoors there's the usual excellent choice of houseplants, and of course a large garden shop with every kind of garden accessory.

Other franchises on this site are listed on a board at the entrance: a quality reproduction English and Italian furniture store; sports wear and goods; a food hall; a freezer centre; Model World; Horse & Country; Banbury Doors & Windows. An arcade of indoor shops sells pine furniture, high-class gifts, needlecraft and candles, carpets and rugs, pets and accessories, and works by local artists.

There is a very good cafeteria (franchised) within the garden centre, and near the approach drive are a pub-cum-restaurant and Chinese restaurant & take-away.

LEEDS CASTLE is just minutes away.

OPEN: 9am to 5:45pm Mon - Sat; 11am to 5pm Sundays.

Aquatics/fish	✔	Information desk	✔
Bookshop	✔	Landscaping service	✘
Car park	✔	Machinery	✔
Conservatories	✔	Ornaments/statues	✔
Clothing	✘	Pets/accessories	✔
Floristry	✔	Play area	✘
Garden furniture	✔	Restaurant/cafeteria	✔
Greenhouses for sale	✔	Sheds etc	✔
Houseplants	✔	Swimming pools	✔

LEEDS CASTLE
nr Maidstone.
Tel: (01622) 765400
Fax: (01622) 735616

"The loveliest castle in the world." Lord Conway's observation would be contested by few of the 500,000 visitors annually from all over the globe. History, romance, architecture, landscaping and entertainment come together to create a uniquely English gem.

There has been a castle on the two islands in the lake since the 9th century. It has been a royal residence to six medieval queens and palace to Henry VIII. But unlike so many castles this has been a happy, comfortable home, not a bleak, imposing fortress; rooms are sumptuous and chockfull of treasures. The famous Culpeper family lived here in the 17th century, from whom the Flower Garden takes its name. This has been carefully planted in recent times on the site of an old kitchen garden, to ensure a splash of colour, fragrance, form and texture throughout the season. It holds two national collections, one of which is catnip – herbs are rather a speciality.

In the rest of the 500 acres of lush parkland are to be found a duckery, home to unusual and exotic wildfowl; a dog collar museum; an aviary with over 100 rare species; Wood and Pavilion Garden – streams, lakes and waterfalls, plus carpets of spring flowers and superb rhododendrons and azaleas; a vineyard; 13 greenhouses; a yew-tree maze, at the heart of which is a grotto taking you into a "world of beasts and legends, tunnels and tumbling water."

It will take at least three hours to see all this, so you may wish to avail yourself of the Fairfax Hall licensed restaurant in a 17th-century barn (there are also picnic sites and fast food outlets in summer). Quality plants and gifts may be purchased in the shops. A full calendar of special events includes a Spring Gardens Week, a flower festival, open air concerts, fireworks, Kentish Evening Dinners (every Saturday except August). For details tel: (01891) 800656. Box office: (01622) 880008.

OPEN: 10am to 5pm* March to October; 10am to 3pm* (* last admission) Nov. to Feb. Closed Christmas Day.
DAYS CLOSED in 1995: June 24, July 1, Nov. 4., prior to special events.

GILLETT COOK GARDEN CENTRE

Monks Granary, Standard Quay,
Faversham.
Tel: (01795) 532235
Fax: (01795) 538868

Very few garden centres can lay claim to 400 years of trading history! Situated alongside Faversham Creek at the bottom of Abbey Street, Gillett Cook were originally merchants and flour millers, delivering to London by sailing barge – several are still tethered alongside and can be viewed when visiting the garden centre. The business still operates from the oldest working granary in the country, built with materials from the abbey in the mid-14th century.

To the rear of the granary the garden centre (HTA) is enclosed by a 12ft high wall, ideal to display a large selection of Clematis and other climbers, and affording shelter to a wide range of shrubs, roses and bedding plants. A good number of china and terra cotta pots are also offered for sale. Management and staff take pride in the level of personal service and advice.

Inside there are no less than 400 varieties of flower and vegetable seeds, plus a full range of insecticides and fungicides. You will also find uncommon New

Zealand Pine furniture. Meander through the granary itself and you will surely find something of interest: country wear, perhaps (a speciality); or animal feed and accessories for all types of livestock; on the first floor are BYGONES – stripped pine, satinwod, brass and iron beds, and many other oddities from the past.

OPEN: 8am to 5pm Mon - Fri; 8am to 4:30pm Sat; 9:30am to 4:30pm Sun.

Aquatics / fish	✗	Information desk	✗
Bookshop	✗	Landscaping service	✗
Car park	✔	Machinery	✗
Conservatories	✗	Ornaments / statues	✔
Clothing	✔	Pets / accessories	✔
Floristry	✗	Play area	✗
Garden furniture	✔	Restaurant / cafeteria	✗
Greenhouses for sale	✗	Sheds etc	✗
Houseplants	✔	Swimming pools	✗

NORTON ASH NURSERY
Norton Crossroads, nr Sittingbourne.
Tel: (01795) 521549

"The Garden of England" is an appropriate epithet, especially when the acres of orchards are in bloom – a spectacular welcome home to Channel Tunnel travellers, in place of the white cliffs.

And it was for fruit that this nursery began 25 years ago, here by the old Roman Road from Dover to London, just a mile or two from Sittingbourne. Today it is a huge self-contained garden and leisure complex, where even non-gardeners can spend a very happy time. In nearly seven acres are to be found a PET GARDEN and leisure area, a MINIATURE RAILWAY, a FARM SHOP, IRONCRAFT & FURNITURE WORKSHOPS, SPECIALIST DOLLS, CHILDREN'S CLOTHING, BONSAI, GIFT & MODEL SHOPS!

That is not to say that the serious gardener has been forgotten: the centre, a member of the HTA and PTIA, stocks a comprehensive range of plants, shrubs and trees, as well as just about every imaginable garden requisite. If you still have time after all this, don't forget lovely Leeds Castle is not far.

Aquatics/fish	✔	Information desk	✔
Bookshop	✘	Landscaping service	✘
Car park	✔	Machinery	✔
Conservatories	✔	Ornaments/statues	✔
Clothing	✔	Pets/accessories	✔
Floristry	✔	Play area	✔
Garden furniture	✔	Restaurant/cafeteria	✔
Greenhouses for sale	✔	Sheds etc	✔
Houseplants	✔	Swimming pools	✘

OPEN: 9am to 5pm Mon - Sat; 11am to 5pm Sundays.

NOTCUTTS GARDEN CENTRE
Guildford Road, Cranleigh.
Tel: (01483) 274222
Fax: (01483) 267247

This is probably the loveliest part of Surrey, a hilly, wooded area of picturesque villages (most celebrated of which is Shere, not far from this Centre). It is also one of the wealthiest areas in Britain, evident from the gracious houses surrounded by gorgeous gardens. No doubt many of the fortunate inhabitants come here, just south of Shamley Green on the B2128 towards Cranleigh, for their garden needs and advice.

Part of the family-owned Notcutts Group, this Centre can call upon the full range of hardy nursery stock grown at Woodbridge, Oxford and nearby Bagshot, over 2,000 varieties attractively presented and clearly marked, as is the hallmark of the group. Planted areas may stimulate ideas or just afford an opporunity to relax a while in a very agreeable location. Or take a break in the restaurant, its sizeable menu listing children's specials.

Garden furniture is a particular strength: a fine selection of teak, resin and upholstered furniture is displayed on a large plinth area. This doubles as a stage for a Christmas fairyland of glittering decora-

tions and lights, with many unusual gifts and Christmas pot plants. Hampers can also be made up from the food shop. There's also a very good pets section, including fish and birds.

OPEN: 8:30am to 5:30pm Mon - Sat;
11am to 5pm Sundays.

Aquatics/fish	✔	Information desk	✔
Bookshop	✔	Landscaping service	✔
Car park	✔	Machinery	✔
Conservatories	✗	Ornaments/statues	✔
Clothing	✔	Pets/accessories	✔
Floristry	✔	Play area	✗
Garden furniture	✔	Restaurant/cafeteria	✔
Greenhouses for sale	✗	Sheds etc	✗
Houseplants	✔	Swimming pools	✗

BIRDWORLD BIRD PARK & GARDENS

Holt Pound, Farnham.
Tel: (01420) 22140
Fax: (01420) 23715

It would be fruitless to debate which is the more important, birds or plants. Here they complement one another to perfection. Our feathered friends are surely the loveliest of all animals, although there are exceptions – the marabou stork is no oil painting. But there are over 1,000 exotic birds calling this home, from penguins to pelicans, parrots to peacocks, and perhaps the most graceful of them all, the flamingoes. It all began as a small bird garden back in 1968, and it is still run personally by the same family (the Harveys) ever since.

The gardens are worth seeing in themselves. Spacious, well laid out and with ample seating, the 25 acres are easy to view at leisure, and the wide paths make for easy access by wheelchair (for hire). Birdworld gardeners Jo Mankelow and Jane Gardner are always happy to advise visitors, and planting is very varied. Some noteworthy features include beautiful bedding systems, tubs and hanging baskets, herbaceous beds, flowering shrubs, many fine trees and an ornamental grass bed.

There is a cafe serving light refreshment and a shop.

OPEN: 9:30am to 6pm (4pm in winter) daily except Christmas Day.

NOTCUTTS GARDEN CENTRE (WATERER'S NURSERIES)
London Road, Bagshot.
Tel: (01276) 472288

A few minutes' walk heading west from the village centre will bring you to this colourful and versatile branch of the esteemed Notcutts Group. Formerly Waterer's Nurseries, it has all the hallmarks of this successful company, plus a few of its own.

The denizens of the pet shop are guaranteed to melt the iciest heart, especially the floppy-eared rabbits. There are numerous other cute rodents (including chipmunks), and some very uncommon birds and tropical fish. Children love it, and it is probably no coincidence that the play area is sited nearby.

The planteria has much to absorb the serious gardener, and labelling is very specific, eg "climbing plants for south-facing walls". Climbers and roses are very well represented; the rose field can be seen to the rear of the site, and indeed many other plants are grown in the nursery for sale. Definitely not grown outside, however, are the exotic ferns, ranging up to £260. Prices are considerably less in the very good 'Special Promotions' section.

The enormous indoor area has all one could ask for and more, including a gift-shop, pantry (selling conserves), cards and good choice of garden furniture. Parts are frequently given over to shows, demonstrations and other events detailed on a calendar which can be picked up by the checkout. Special mention must go to the Rhododendron Festival in May and the marvellous Christmas Grotto, with Santa dispensing his jollity to children free of charge.

OPEN: 9am to 5:30pm (6pm in Spring) Mon - Sat; 11am to 5pm Sundays.

Aquatics / fish	✔	Landscaping design	
Bookshop	✔	service	✔
Car park	✔	Machinery (limited)	✔
Conservatories	✔	Ornaments / statues	✔
Clothing	✔	Pets / accessories	✔
Floristry	✔	Play area	✔
Garden furniture	✔	Restaurant / cafeteria	✔
Greenhouses for sale	✔	Sheds etc	✔
Houseplants	✔	Swimming pools	✔
Information desk	✔		

THE SAVILL GARDEN
Wick Lane, Englefield Green,
nr Egham.
Tel: (01753) 860222 (enquiries);
(01784) 435544 (entrance)
Fax: (01753) 859617;
tel: (01784) 432326 (restaurant)

Windsor Great Park is known the world over, but sometimes overlooked is that within its 4,500 acres is one of the finest temperate gardens of its kind anywhere. Begun in 1932 by the late Sir Eric Savill, in close co-operation with King George VI and the Queen Mother, these 35 acres contain much to absorb the keen plantsman as well as the simple lover of nature.

Considering the sandy soil and exceptionally dry climate, the garden represents a major achievement. Whatever the season, the visitor is rewarded with a display of colour. Lovely camellias, magnolias, rhododendrons and azaleas (especially when reflected in the waters) light up the spring, when daffodils are also of great importance. Primulas, meconopsis, hostas and ferns flourish in the moist woodland. Lilies and hydrangeas adorn the summer months, and this is the best time to see the formal garden, where there are hundreds of modern roses, extensive herbaceous borders, a range of alpines and the new

'Dry Garden' featuring plants from the Mediterranean and other quite arid parts of the globe. Autumn sees a whole new tapestry of marvellous colours and fruits, and even winter has much to commend it.

Other attractions include a number of ponds linked by streams, a New Zealand collection, an arboretum, willow garden and Alpine meadow. Endangered plants are a priority of the management, Crown Estates, which also takes pride in clear labelling.

The self-serve restaurant is licensed (there's also a lakeside picnic site); it is closed from Dec.18th to Jan. 8th. Adjacent to the GIFT/BOOKSHOP, the PLANT CENTRE is very well stocked. Take time to visit VALLEY GARDENS, just one mile away.

OPEN: 10am to 6pm March - Oct, 10am to 4pm Nov - Feb, daily except Christmas & Boxing Days. Guided tours by arrangement.

NOTCUTTS GARDEN CENTRE
Staines Road, Laleham
Tel: (01784) 460832

This is the most recent addition to the Notcutts' stable, acquired only in April 1994. Already it bears the stamp of this highly regarded and growing group, and many more developments are in the pipeline.

First impressions are of great spaciousness – over five acres in all – especially valuable in a built-up suburban area such as this, just a few miles from Heathrow Airport. The vast under-cover shop is exceptionally light and airy, its open-plan roominess lending itself to relaxed and unhurried browsing. Here you will find most garden accessories, plus cards, gifts and a good range of glassware. A separate franchise stocks an excellent range of lawn mowers and other machinery, as well as mountain bikes. Apart from high quality boots there was no clothing at time of writing.

At the far end of the building is a pleasant cafeteria, which has a terrace overlooking a beautifully landscaped pond with ornamental bridge. Here one can contentedly while away some time over a coffee and a snack, flicking through a catalogue, watching the great airliners float up noiselessly from the airport, or allowing the eyes to rest on the whale-sized koi (not for sale) in the crystal-clear waters – a little piece of rural tranquility not far from the M3 and M25. Thus inspired, one will find aquatic plants (but not fish at the moment) sited adjacent.

The planteria is laid out in rows and well labelled. All own-grown, shrubs are a speciality. To the rear is a range of Robinsons greenhouses and conservatories, and other garden buildings include novelty sheds.

OPEN: 9am to 6pm (5pm in winter)
Mon -Sat; 11am to 5pm Sundays.

Aquatics	✔	Information desk	✔
Bookshop	✔	Landscaping service	✗
Car park	✔	Machinery	✔
Conservatories	✔	Ornaments/statues	✔
Clothing	✗	Pet accessories	✔
Floristry	✗	Play area	✗
Garden furniture	✔	Restaurant/cafeteria	✔
Greenhouses for sale	✔	Sheds etc	✔
Houseplants	✔	Swimming pools	✗

AIRPORT AQUARIA

**Heathrow Garden Centre,
Sipson Road, West Drayton.
Tel: 0181 897 2563
Fax: 0181 897 2563**

Heathrow is the world's greatest airport, so naturally road connections are excellent. Apart from travellers, many people drive some distance just to watch the great jets landing and taking off, to experience some of the excitement or enjoy the facilities of the airport.

But tucked away just a short drive from the main terminals remains a little patch of the original countryside, surprisingly quiet considering the proximity. From junction 4 of the M4 follow the signs for Sipson (passing under the motorway). Just past the Forte Crest Hotel is a cottagey little pub (The Plough), next to which is the Heathrow Garden Centre. Although a separate entity, Airport Aquaria is situated by its entrance.

In limited space this privately-run centre has, over 15 years, sold one of the largest selections of high-quality pond plants in the south of England. It has attended all the major garden shows, including Chelsea and Hampton

Court. Many of the plants are rarely seen elsewhere, but they are all clearly labelled and arranged according to type, eg Deep Marginals or Oxygenating. Alongside are several tanks of healthy-looking coldwater fish. Some uncommon varieties can be seen inside, and there is also a tropical aquarium. All the paraphernalia associated with ponds – pumps, lights, filters, fish foods and other related products are stocked.

Special mention must be made of the increasingly popular self-contained water features. An exclusive collection called "Waterways" is available from Airport Aquaria, or by MAIL ORDER. Amongst these are spouting mill-stones, mushroom and cobbles fountains, Ali Baba spouting vases, wall fountains, drilled and weeping rocks. Even the smallest garden can accommodate them, and will be enhanced by the movement and sound of splashing water. They are also much less costly than a full blown pond or fountain – ask for a catalogue and price list.

OPEN: 9am to 6pm every day in summer, 10am to 4pm every day in winter.

P. J. Bridgman & Co. Ltd. Barnbridge Works, Lockfield Ave, Brimsdown, Enfield, Middlesex EN3 7PX, England Tel: 0181-804 7474   Fax: 0181-805 0873

SOUTH OCKENDEN GARDEN CENTRE
**South Road (B186), South Ockenden.
Tel: (01708) 851991**

A reputation has been well earned at The Chelsea Flower Show for prize-winning hanging baskets, and demonstrations are given by the centre's own experts during April and May. The Plant House is another award-winning attraction, with an outstanding choice of houseplants, which are delivered two or three times a week. Outdoor plants are also of the highest quality, and there's a strong ethic of courtesy from the friendly staff.

The 'Fishy Friends' shop is a watery paradise for the enthusiast, and children will also love the pet area, which has rabbits, goats and donkeys. The gift and book shop always has an excellent choice (and wrapping service), but becomes extra special at Christmas when Father Christmas is in attendance. The coffee shop serves various fresh home-made cakes and snacks – sandwiches are filled to order.

Apart from all this there is also a programme of events, which include auctions, children's shows, egg hunt at Easter, demonstrations and excursions – ask for a leaflet.

Access from the M25 is very easy, and Europe's largest indoor shopping centre, Lakeside, is very near.

OPEN: 9am to 6pm, Mon - Sat; 10:30am to 4:30pm Sundays.

Aquatics/fish	✔	Ornaments/statues	✔
Bookshop	✔	Pets/accessories	✔
Car park	✔	Play area	✔
Garden furniture	✔	Restaurant/cafeteria	✔
Greenhouses for sale	✔	Sheds etc	✔
Houseplants	✔		
Machinery	✔	✱ Calor Gas main dealer	

ESSEX WATER SYSTEMS
37 Harold Gardens, Wickford,
SS11 7EP.
Tel & Fax: (01268) 765218

With the droughts of recent years and the installation of water meters looking ever more likely, now is the time to look closely at conserving water. Our efficient and cost-effective garden watering systems use up to 70% less water than old-fashioned methods where water is thrown into the air via hosepipes or sprinklers.

Porous Pipe is a soaker hose made from recycled car tyres. British made, this is the only one that will run off the mains or directly from a water butt using stored water. Porous Pipe really is the easy, lazy and most efficient way to water your garden or greenhouse: just a turn of the tap is all that is needed. We also supply a system, unique to Essex Water Systems, for watering all your tubs and hanging baskets simultaneously.

Also available:-

* Water diverters for diverting rainwater or bathwater into your water butt or tank; suitable for square or round down pipes, in a range of colours.

* Holiday watering kits to water the garden in your absence.

* Pumps for garden use with mains voltage, or 12 volts DC with own power source – ideal for moving stored water around the garden.

* Water features for the conservatory or garden.

We have years of experience in supplying cost-effective and efficient watering systems to the domestic and commercial markets. All our systems can be installed DIY, or we offer a complete installation service if required. Advice always available.

THE ALTERNATIVE
TO HOSING YOUR
GARDEN

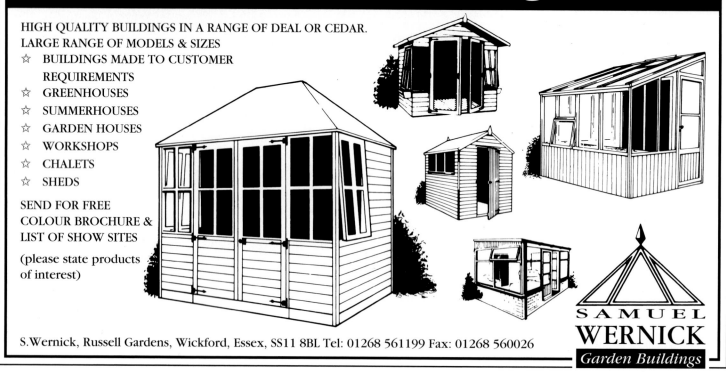

BYPASS NURSERIES
72 Ipswich Road, Colchester.
Tel: (01206) 865500

Traditionally these nurseries have enjoyed international repute for growing primroses, but are employing the same skills to expand fast into other areas, and now stock a wide selection of sometimes weird but always wonderful plants. 1994 saw the introduction of a large range of Primula Auriculas, Penstemons, argyranthemums and many other worthies. Plans for new ranges are made two or three years in advance, to keep ahead of the competition, always with garden-worthiness, quality and value in mind. Stocks are continually replenished to ensure peak condition. Manager Gina Zimmerman and staff are energetically keen to help you choose – those working in the water garden section are described as "pond-nutty!"

Pensioners should join the Senior Gardeners Club, which entitles them to a midweek discount, special evenings and lots of other goodies. The centre is also 'wheelchair-friendly.'

To find the centre, follow the A1232 off the A12 towards Colchester for about two miles to a double roundabout. Go straight over and take the first right. There are numerous other attractions to make a full day out: you will be right in the heart of Constable Country, and the sister centre at Capel St Mary (see opposite) is not far.

OPEN: normal hours, every day.

Aquatics/fish	✔	Information desk	✔
Bookshop	✔	Landscaping service	✗
Car park	✔	Machinery	✗
Conservatories	✔	Ornaments/statues	✔
Clothing	✗	Pets/accessories	✔
Floristry	✔	Play area	✗
Garden furniture	✔	Restaurant/cafeteria	✗
Greenhouses for sale	✔	Sheds etc	✔
Houseplants	✔	Swimming pools	✗

NOTCUTTS GARDEN CENTRE
**Station Road, Ardleigh, nr Colchester.
(signposted from village centre)
Tel: (01206) 230271**

The smallest of the group, this Centre nonetheless carries the full range of plants and dry goods, and, located in a nice little valley right next to a railway crossing, is also very pleasantly laid out for visitors. The car park is bordered by unusual demonstration hedges, helpfully labelled, and on entering one is further guided by signs showing plants suitable for shade, for example. The planteria is very colourful in summer, bedecked with hanging baskets and at its centre is an eye-catching patio feature. Rhododendrons are especially good, but there is particular pride in the cold water fish and pond plants section, one of the best in the area. The shop carries some excellent garden furniture, plus houseplants, ceramics and much else.

*OPEN: 8:30am to 5:30pm Mon - Sat;
11am to 5pm Sundays.*

Aquatics /fish	✔	Garden furniture	✔	Ornaments /statues	✔
Bookshop	✔	Greenhouses for sale	✘	Pets /accessories	✘
Car park	✔	Houseplants	✔	Play area	✔
Conservatories	✘	Information desk	✔	Restaurant /cafeteria	✘
Clothing	✘	Landscaping service	✘	Sheds etc	✘
Floristry	✘	Machinery	✔	Swimming pools	✘

BYPASS NURSERIES
Old London Road, Capel St Mary, nr Ipswich.
Tel: (01473) 310604

"Bringing the gardener even closer to growing" – says manager Tessa Reeves. She speaks literally, for the centre is attached to one of the nurseries, so plants have only a very short journey to make. Thus one may be confident they are in prime condition.

Much research has gone into the plant selection: from geraniums which drop their seed heads after flowering (conveniently dead-heading themselves), to the stunningly beautiful trailing Balcon geraniums, to the huge range of hanging baskets and trailing plants. Not only are the best varieties selected, but also the individual plants from which to propagate. There is such enormous diversity within species that one must painstakingly seek out those truest to form. Customers' comments are always welcome in the endeavour for greater things!

All the usual garden sundries are stocked, and it is policy to keep prices as low as possible. Further reductions are available midweek to members of the Senior Gardeners Club, as well as special evenings and other perks. The centre is also 'wheelchair-friendly'.

Take the Capel St Mary exit off the A12, in the heart of Constable Country. Also visit the sister branch nearby (see opposite). Both members of HTA, each with its own character.

OPEN: normal hours, every day.

Aquatics/fish	✘	Landscaping service	✘
Bookshop	✔	Machinery	✘
Car park	✔	Ornaments/statues	✔
Conservatories	✔	Pets/accessories	✔
Clothing	✘	Play area	✔
Floristry	✔	Restaurant/cafeteria	✔
Garden furniture	✔	(Happy Eater)	
Greenhouses for sale	✔	Sheds etc	✔
Houseplants	✔	Swimming pools	✔
Information desk	✔		

LETTS SWIMMING POOLS LTD
Semer, Hadleigh, nr Ipswich.
Tel: (01473) 822375
Fax: (01473) 824223

Over 70% of Letts' pools are built on the recommendation of previous clients, many of whom have taken the trouble to express their appreciation in writing. This, plus the fact that the company has been in the business since 1965, is eloquent enough testimonial, especially given the vagaries of the British economy and climate.

Still privately owned, the company was formed by Gordon Letts, who had 10 years previous experience in the horticultural trade and 12 as a landscape architect. Now it is son Richard who carries on the tradition of craftsmanship, quality and customer care (member of SPATA and Guild of Master Craftsmen). He personally gives each quotation – no reps – and deals only in the best products. Similarly, construction staff are all qualified, experienced and full time (no sub-contractors), ensuring not only a high standard but also speed of execution.

Letts operate only within the region (which helps with after sales service), and have built many hundreds of pools in all shapes and sizes, ranging from small

domestics up to 25-metre lengths for schools, hospitals, clubs etc. All types of enclosure, from economy plastic types to a full luxurious brick and timber building, are well within their competence. Apart from the standard designs, Letts are also happy to meet clients' individual requirements, with special regard to exisitng features – correct siting is very important in the first place, as is landscaping once the job is done.

Fully guaranteed, the pools are constructed of steel-reinforced concrete, and finished internally with polished 'Marbleite' and mosaic tiles at water level, endowing the water with a lovely translucent pale blue effect. They can also be laid on the floor. The coping stone serves as a hand grip.

Heavy duty pumps and filters keep the water clear, and Letts will also supply various forms of heating and lighting, diving boards, cleaning devices and chemicals, or even a sauna bath. A large stock of spares means that servicing work is quick and efficient. If, however, you feel you can do it all yourself, they will be happy to supply a construction kit and the necessary advice.

The demonstration pool and showrooms at Semer (just north of Hadleigh) are open from 9am to 5pm Monday to Friday, other times by appointment.

NOTCUTTS GARDEN CENTRE
Ipswich Road, Woodbridge.
Tel: (01394) 383344

Winner of 'England in Bloom' competition and one of East Anglia's prettiest small towns, Woodbridge is a natural home for Notcutts; established 95 years, this is the original and is still head office. Tucked into a little dell (with a stream) and beautifully landscaped, the Centre is a pleasure to stroll around. Mature trees and rather nice rose borders provide the backdrop to a well-stocked planteria, including a patio feature. Don't miss the bargain plants (to be found at all Notcutts Centres), or the many hanging baskets, ablaze with colour in high summer. The shop also has much worth seeing, including furniture of a very high standard, houseplants and every other conceivable gardening requisite. As always, there is an information kiosk, but you may also like to ask about the landscaping service, especially having seen what they've done with the dell.

Near to both river and town, Notcutts should be part of your itinerary for a very enjoyable day in Woodbridge.

OPEN: 8:30am to 5:30pm Mon - Sat;
11am to 5pm Sundays.

Aquatics	✔	Information desk	✔
Bookshop	✔	Landscaping service	✔
Car park	✔	Machinery	✔
Conservatories	✘	Ornaments/statues	✔
Clothing	✘	Pets/accessories	✘
Floristry	✘	Play area	✔
Garden furniture	✔	Restaurant/cafeteria	✘
Greenhouses for sale	✘	Sheds etc	✘
Houseplants	✔	Swimming pools	✘

SOVEREIGN TURF
**Fir Tree Farm, Blaxhall, nr
Woodbridge.
Tel: (01728) 688984
Fax: (01728) 688949**

Sovereign Turf is a Suffolk-based company specialising in the growing of high quality cultivated turf for the sports and amenity markets.

All turf is grown on a light sand, the optimum medium for turf production, endowing it with unique properties unobtainable in any other soil. It is light, easy to handle and, with careful selection of each grass species, produces turf of outstanding quality: weed-free, disease-resistant and green all year round.

Each grade of turf is grown for specific situations: domestic lawns turf is hard wearing, able to withstand intensive use by children and animals, and therefore ideally suited for back garden lawns; ornamental lawns turf is to be preferred where there is less wear and tear – the front lawn, perhaps – and is characteristically more prestigious in appearance, although still quite resilient.

Whilst growing mainly for the large scale users, Sovereign Turf recognise that domestic users will usually require smaller amounts, so make it available through the folllowing selected outlets:-

The Garden Centre
**Garden Farm
Blofield
nr Norwich
Tel: (0603) 715034**

Early Dawn Nurseries
**Rushmere Road
Carlton Colville
nr Lowestoft
Tel: (0502) 476340**

L. Swann Nursery
**A1152 Bentwaters Road
Bromeswell
nr Woodbridge
(0394) 382698**

Each has turf on display so you can decide which you prefer. Information is also available on how you might prepare the site for laying turf, getting the grass established, and maintaining the lawn to a high standard throughout the year.

Sovereign Turf is used extensively throughout eastern England both for private gardens and large scale projects. IPSWICH TOWN FOOTBALL CLUB and WIMBLEDON LAWN TENNIS CLUB number amongst the more prestigious customers.

Lawn by Sovereign Turf

FISK'S CLEMATIS NURSERY
Westleton, nr Saxmundham.
Tel: (01728) 648263

The name of Fisk is synonymous with the clematis. Founder Jim Fisk is the author of the RHS booklet on the subject, and of "Clematis, the Queen of Climbers" currently in paperback at £12.99.

It all began just after the Second World War. Mr Fisk left the navy with £80 and went to work in his brother's garden growing clematis for a nursery in Leicester where he had been a propagator before the war. He took a post round to help ends meet! Now next to his home, the nursery today has several tunnel houses, three large glass houses and grows about 20,000 plants per year.

The nursery has exhibited at the Chelsea Flower Show for 30 years and has introduced many new varieties, some named after friends and colleagues. They are amongst 150, several very unusual, listed in an exceptionally informative catalogue. They are available by mail order and come with careful instructions, but a visit to the nursery itself would be most rewarding. The display gardens are full of all kinds of blooms you are unlikely to see elsewhere, from early spring to late autumn - a true demonstration of the versatility and value of this favourite climber. Westleton is a very pleasant village, adjacent to Minsmere Nature Reserve and midway between Felixstowe and Yarmouth on this Heritage Coast.

OPEN: 9am to 5pm weekdays, 10am to 1pm and 2pm to 5pm Saturdays and Sundays in summer.

EARLY DAWN NURSERIES
Rushmere Road, Carlton Colville, nr Lowestoft.
Tel: (01502) 476340
Fax: (01502) 476887

The name is appropriate enough, out here at Britain's most easterly extreme, the first to see the morning sun. Although one of the sunniest parts of the country, the east coast can be bitterly cold in winter (and sometimes in summer!), so a conservatory is especially desirable here, both for personal comfort and to house tender and exotic plants.

And it is the conservatories which first catch the eye on entering this unusual and pleasantly laid out garden centre. They are all manufactured and erected by the same company which owns the centre (and also makes windows, sealed units etc), so the choice is exceptional, quality and service assured. Portable buildings and sheds are also supplied.

Having been 21 years a wholesale nursery, company roots are still firmly in the growing of plants; climbers, shrubs and conifers are particular specialities. A member of the NFU and HTA, it still supplies the wholesale market, as well as Leeds, London and Birmingham flower markets. All kinds of landscape work,

domestic and commercial, are undertaken.

The centre is a little of the beaten track, but worth seeking out. Combine, perhaps with a day at the coast or on the nearby Broads.

OPEN: 7:30am to 6:30pm, every day.

Aquatics	✔	Information desk	✔
Bookshop	✔	Landscaping service	✔
Car park	✔	Machinery	✗
Conservatories	✔	Ornaments/statues	✔
Clothing	✔	Pets/accessories	✔
Floristry	✔	Play area	✗
Garden furniture	✔	Restaurant/cafeteria	✗
Greenhouses for sale	✔	Sheds etc	✔
Houseplants	✔	Swimming pools	✗

SOMERLEYTON HALL
Somerleyton, nr Lowestoft.
Tel: (01502) 730224

"For there summer is to be seen in the depths of winter" – the words of historian William Fuller, commenting on the aptness of the name of this lovely estate. He spoke them in 1651, when the wealth of evergreens, then something of a novelty, caused others to marvel too.

But the garden as we see it today is largely a Victorian creation. Even in those times horse-drawn coaches would bring visitors by the thousand, and it is recorded that in 1920 over 8,000 people came here, despit the lack of public transport.

An ever-popular attraction is the yew hedge maze, one of the finest in Britain, designed by William Nestfield and planted in 1846. Another unusual feature is the 300-foot iron pergola, forming a delightful tunnel to walk through, especially when the wisteria is in bloom.

The gardens are ablaze with rhododendrons and azaleas in spring, while in summer it is the herbaceous borders which come into their own. The magnificent trees and shrubs (including a monkey puzzle) can be enjoyed at any time.

Some very fine statues are dotted around the grounds, and on the lawn to the west of the house stands a great equatorial sundial encircled by the signs of the Zodiac. Also of note are the glasshouses by Sir Joseph Paxton, designer of Crystal Palace.

As well as the maze, children will love the aviary and the miniature railway. Parents will appreciate the exceptionally agreeable tearooms, located in a pleasnt winter garden.

Incidentally, the beautiful early-Victorian house once belonged to Sir Morton Peto, builder of the Houses of Parliament and Nelson's Column. The current owners are Lord and Lady Somerleyton.

OPEN: 2pm to 5:30pm Thursdays, Sundays & Bank Hols, from Easter Sunday to September; Tuesdays & Wednesdays also in July & August. House open.

RAVENINGHAM GARDENS
Raveningham, near Loddon.
Tel: (01508) 548222
Fax: (01508) 548958

"Obviously a plantsman's garden, but far more than that, it composes a picture: that of everyone's idea of a country house garden, unaffected by trendy fashions." Country Life's observation is spot on. Perhaps it is in part because this is very much a 'lived in' garden, as witnessed by footballs, tank engines and other things important to schoolboys strewn about.

Areas of the original 18th-century gardens still remain, but most of the planting has taken place over the past 45 to 50 years. There has been mass planting of herbaceous borders, rose gardens and trees, with a strong leaning towards rare and unusual species. The work goes on: former melon pits, a Victorian conservatory and kitchen garden are being revived. The original Victorian conservatory houses many uncommon plants, including a huge variety of geraniums, but it is the cascades of Jasmine and scented climbers which are responsible for the delicious fragrance.

Some surprisingly tender species thrive here, and the delightful walled garden offers extra protection. Many are propagated for sale in the nursery, which stands on merit as first rate in itself, selling over 1,000 varieties of shrubs, trees and herbaceous plants. Raveningham is especially well known for its wide range of Agapanthus and Euphorbias.

Plans for the future include a herb garden, arboretum, magnolias and more shrubs. We mortals only see a snapshot of a garden: it is a living, ever-changing thing.

One of our best and most time-honoured traditions, envied around the world, is home made tea in an English country garden. There can be few finer places in which to enjoy one. Guided tours, with light refreshment, can be laid on for groups, and coach parties are welcome.

OPEN: Garden mid-March to mid-September, Wednesdays 1pm to 4pm, Sundays and Bank Hols 2pm to 5pm. NURSERY: Monday - Friday 9am to 5pm all year (plus Saturday from March to October); Sundays and Bank Hols 2pm to 5pm mid-March to mid-September.

NB: GATE & TEAROOM RECEIPTS GO TO CHARITIES (incl. Red Cross, St John Ambulance, Dr Barnardo's).

NOTCUTTS GARDEN CENTRE
Daniels Road, Norwich.
(ring road, between A11 and A140)
Tel: (01603) 53155

There has been a nursery on this site since 1844, and it was acquired from Daniels Bros in 1976. Since then it has become established as one of Norfolk's leading Centres, its huge car park sometimes over-flowing into an adjacent field. In common with all Notcutts centres it has a planteria (outstanding for rhododendrons and shrubs), well-stocked dry goods shop and first grade houseplants (some real bargains on offer), plus children's play area and information kiosk. But in addition are a superb floristry section (including wonderful artificial and dried flowers), and a pets and aquatic centre housed with the coffee shop. The latter is franchised, as are garden buildings, swimming pools and wood-burning stoves. For its range of plants this Notcutts has few equals, and there's also a fine bookshop and some real quality wooden furniture.

*OPEN: 8:30am to 5:30pm Mon - Sat;
11am to 5pm Sundays.*

Aquatics/fish	✔	Information desk	✔
Bookshop	✔	Landscaping service	✗
Car park	✔	Machinery	✔
Conservatories	✔	Ornaments/statues	✔
Clothing	✗	Pets/accessories	✔
Floristry	✔	Play area	✔
Garden furniture	✔	Restaurant/cafeteria	✔
Greenhouses for sale	✔	Sheds etc	✔
Houseplants	✔	Swimming pools	✔

THE FAIRHAVEN GARDEN TRUST

South Walsham, nr Norwich.
Tel: (01603) 270449

The Norfolk Broads provide a very special habitat for both flora and fauna. The gardens of Fairhaven make the very best use of its natural assets . . . nature perfected, says resident warden and manager George Debbage, who has worked here since 1963 when it was part of Lord Fairhaven's South Walsham Hall Estate.

As one would expect, water is the key element in these restful gardens – they lie beside the private South Walsham Inner Broad, fingers of which intrude well into the natural woodland. Tree-lined walks next to the calm waters are a joy at any time of the year, but especially so in the autumn – look for the 900-year-old King Oak. In spring the rhododendrons and azaleas take full advantage of the acidic soil to put on a marvellous show, and primulas, giant lilies, rare shrubs and other plants, plus many native wild flowers, also thrive. But perhaps pride of place should go to the Candelabra Primula, which in May carpets in red, white and pink the marshy woodland between the raised paths.

These and other plants may be purchased.

Treat yourself to a river trip on 'The Lady Beatrice,' a vintage-style river boat which glides from the gardens every half-hour.

For a small extra fee you may also like to visit the BIRD SANCTUARY.

Back at the entrance is a TEA ROOM, small shop and information desk. Large groups and coach parties must be pre-booked, and guided walks can also be arranged.

OPEN: 11am to 6pm weekdays & Sundays, 2pm to 6pm Saturdays; closed Mondays except Bank Hols. SPECIAL DATES: Primrose weekend mid-April; Candelabra Primula Weekend 3rd week in May; Autumn Colours Week last week in October.

HOVETON HALL GARDENS
Wroxham, nr Norwich.
Tel: (01603) 782798
Fax: (01603) 784564

Purists will say that, being on the north side of the river (just off the A1151), these gardens are actually in Hoveton, not Wroxham, but what is not in doubt is that they are 10 acres of very fine Broadland gardens – a 'paradise discovered.'

The sizeable lake in front of the house is fed by streams, around which is planted a unique combination of plants, shrubs and trees. Spring is the best time to see this, when the glorious show of countless daffodils of many varieties is closely followed by the splendour of rhododendrons and azaleas, flourishing in the moist, acidic soil.

In summer the herbaceous borders come into their own, a chance to see many uncommon plants as well as the reliable favourites. These are contained within the walled 'Spider Garden,' so named on account of the extraordinary circular iron gate fashioned in the form of a spider's web. There's also a walled Victorian Kitchen Garden where plants are for sale.

The Woodland Walk could be accompanied by the song of many types of bird. A walk by the lakeside is always a pleasure, and as well as the waterfowl you will see magnificent specimens of Royal Fern, Gunnera, many Hostas, Euphorbias and Candelabra Primulas. Numerous species of butterfly also frequent the gardens – you may even glimpse a White Admiral.

Light refreshments are available in converted farm buildings, and books and cards are also sold. Other gardening publications may be obtained on request, even if rare or out of print.

OPEN: 11am to 5:30pm Wednesdays, Fridays, Sundays & Bank Hols, from Easter Sunday to mid-September. House not open. Dogs not permited.

BLICKLING HALL & GARDEN
Blickling, nr Aylsham.
Tel: (01263) 733084
Fax: (01263) 734924

First-time visitors invariably exhale a gasp of admiration as this striking Jacobean mansion suddenly hoves into view in a break in the trees. It is one of East Anglia's finest and most historic buildings, and also one of the very first in the land to be acquired by the National Trust. The interior matches expectations, and neither will the gardens disappoint.

To the east of the house is an extensive parterre with large, exotic herbacous borders, best seen in July and August. A month or two earlier the rhododendrons and azaleas hold centre stage with their great swathes of dazzling colour. Not far away you'll stumble upon the delightful Secret Garden and an 18th-century orangery. The dry moat is home to a broad range of colourful plants, while to the south are the great yew hedges planted in the 17th century. Every great house must have its lake, and this one is around a mile long and crescent-shaped. A pyramidal mausoleum is one of the unusual buildings lurking in the grounds. Miles of paths and bridleways thread their way through the park and woods.

Right at the gates, the Buckinghamshire Arms (with accommodation) is one of the best known pubs in the area, and the Hall also has a restaurant, picnic area and shop. A PLANT CENTRE, featuring the 'Blickling Collections,' occupies the old orchard.

OPEN: 11am to 5pm daily except Mons & Thurs from end of March to end of October. Open Bank Hols but not Good Friday. Gardens open every day during July & August.

WATTON GARDEN CENTRE
Norwich Road, Watton, nr Thetford.
Tel & Fax: (01953) 881195

The tea room is worth a visit in itself: opened by the new owner at Easter '94, it is very tastefully appointed in the style of a garden room and spotlessly clean – certainly a cut above the norm for morning coffee, lunch or afternon tea.

Further developments are afoot, first among which is a children's play area, planned at time of writing. Waste ground behind the site will doubtless soon be put to good use, but meanwhile there is still much worth seeing at this relatively compact and notably friendly centre. The patio section (pictured) is a particularly good one, fencing and timber products are of prime quality, and all the garden furniture is wooden.

But the motto is "Run by plantsmen for plantsmen" and indeed all plants are well laid out and labelled, shrubs and perennials being the forte. Interesting features are the 'rooms' for hanging baskets, geraniums, strawberries and others, all under cover.

The shop sells most garden requisites, plus extras like books, conserves, dried flowers, some giftware etc. The clothing section is due for expansion.

Aquatics	✔	Landscaping service	✔
Bookshop	✔	Machinery	✘
Car park	✔	Ornaments/statues	
Conservatories	✔	(limited)	✔
Clothing (limited)	✔	Pets/accessories	✘
Floristry	✘	Play area	✔
Garden furniture	✔	Restaurant/cafeteria	✔
Greenhouses for sale	✔	Sheds etc	✔
Houseplants	✔	Swimming pools	✘
Information desk	✔		

OPEN: 9am to 5:30pm, Mon - Sat;
10:30am to 5pm Sundays & Bank Hols.

WAVENEY FISH FARM
Park Road, Diss.
Tel: (01379) 642697

The demonstration gardens here are a marvellous example of what can be achieved in a modest amount of space without the advantage of a spectacular setting – in other words, a typical garden. David Laughlin has created a mini wonderland of rock pools (full of huge koi), cascades, fountains, ornamental bridges and windmills that is a delight on the eye and inspiration to water gardeners.

A pond does add an extra dimension or two to a garden: water plants are very easy to grow and produce some wonderful blooms all through the season; fish are an attraction in themselves, and you will find they are soon joined by a host of frogs, irridescent dragon and damsel flies, the ubiquitous pond skaters and maybe even a water vole or two. In addition, a fountain or cascade adds sound and movement.

Waveney Fish Farm stocks everything you might need to create either a simple pond or a fantasy-like grotto: ornaments and statues, liners, filter systems, pumps, indeed all the hardware, plus an excellent range of fish and container-grown plants. Most important of all is the helpful expert advice to help you get started in this specialist area of gardening. Th centre is a member of the H.T.A. and O.F.I (Ornamental Fish Industries association).

Inside are books and leaflets, accessories and dry goods, an exotic bird and reptile room and tropical fish aquaria. It's almost like a miniature zoo! Children are as enthusiastic as their parents, and a family could have a very pleasant day out. Diss is an agreeable small market town built around a lake (or mere, as it's called here), and the famous Bressingham Gardens and Steam Museum are just a mile or two up the road.

OPEN: 10am to 5pm every day. Closed 1pm to 2pm Mon - Fri. Located on A1066 opp. Park Hotel.

BRESSINGHAM GARDENS, STEAM MUSEUM & PLANT CENTRE

Bressingham, nr Diss.

Tel: (01379) 687386/382
Dell Garden & Steam
(01379) 688133/687464
Plant Centre
(01379) 687464
Mail Order Catalogue

Father and son, Alan and Adrian Bloom have made an inestimable contribution to gardening in this country – indeed, their reputation extends well beyond these shores – and between them have written numerous books and appeared regularly on television and radio.

Alan Bloom moved to this site in 1946, and began the establishment of one of England's most important and best-known gardens, as well as a major nursery and PLANT CENTRE The Steam Museum (a separate entity) would at first appear to be a curious association, and could never have happened had it been planned, but actually the unique blend of visual appeal and a nostalgic atmosphere has worked to make this one of the region's top attractions.

From the earliest days herbaceous

perennials have been the forte. Nowhere will you see these displayed to better advantage than Alan Bloom's most celebrated creation, the magical "DELL GARDEN." Set in the rolling five-acre park in front of Bressingham Hall, over 5,000 varieties (including over 170 raised and named by Alan himself) grace the dell with an inspiring mix of colour, texture and scent, framed by many superb mature trees and shrubs. Adrian Bloom regularly opens his wonderful six-acre private garden, "FOGGY BOTTOM."

It was with hardy perennials that Alan Bloom pioneered the concept of 'island beds', and his innovative skills and imagination extend to hard landscape features, such as bridge, summerhouse and retaining walls, predominantly in Norfolk flint.

In short, Bressingham is a paradise for gardeners (with the boon of being able to purchase much of what they see at the nearby nursery or Plant Centre, or via a comprehensive catalogue) and a sensual treat for anyone who appreciates beauty.

An overnight stay at Bressingham Hall means you can enjoy it all over again the next day!

OPEN: Plant Centre 10am to 5:30pm daily except Christmas Day & Boxing Day. Dell Garden & Steam from April to Sept. Foggy Bottom Mondays only plus 1st Sunday of each month from April to Sept.

NOTCUTTS GARDEN CENTRE
**Oundle Road (A605), Orton Waterville, Peterborough.
(at entrance to Nene Park Nature Reserve)
Tel: (01733) 234600**

The newest of Notcutts' East Anglian quartet, this one is perhaps the most attractively laid out. Designed with the family in mind, the Centre has a good children's play area, restaurant serving hot meals and snacks all day, and a pets and aquatic centre. The 'serious' gardener will find the ususal comprehensive range of plants, trees and shrubs for which

Notcutts is noted, and expert guidance dispensed from an advice centre. In addition, dotted round the site are swimming pools, garden buildings and conservatories, and of course an excellent garden shop selling furniture, lovely houseplants and much else besides. Why not combine with a visit to adjacent Nene Park Nature Reserve?

OPEN: 8:30am to 5:30pm Mon - sat; 11am to 5pm Sundays.

Aquatics/fish	✔	Information desk	✔
Bookshop	✔	Landscaping service	✔
Car park	✔	Machinery	✔
Conservatories	✔	Ornaments/statues	✔
Clothing	✗	Pets/accessories	✔
Floristry	✗	Play area	✔
Garden furniture	✔	Restaurant/cafeteria	✔
Greenhouses for sale	✔	Sheds etc	✔
Houseplants	✔	Swimming pools	✔

FERRY HILL NURSERY & GARDEN CENTRE
134 London Road, Chatteris.
Tel: (01354) 693937

The coffee shop would do credit to many a smart restaurant, but there are other good reasons for a visit to Ferry Hill, a mile or so south of Chatteris in the heart of Fenland. 50% of the plants are home grown, and a comprehensive range includes some quite uncommon – requests can also usually be accommodated, and specialist advice is always to hand from qualified staff. There's also a very fair selection of indoor plants and hanging baskets, whilst at the other end of site is the water garden and ornaments (pictured). Every kind of 'hardware' is here: tools, garden machinery and furniture, paving and walling, plus greenhouses, sheds and conservatories. Make a day of it and take the family; there's a play area for the kids and floristry service for the ladies.

OPEN: 9am to 5:30pm Mon - Fri; 10:30am to 4:30pm Sundays. COFFEE SHOP 10:30am to 4:30pm Wed - Sun.

Aquatics / fish	✔	Information desk	✔
Bookshop	✔	Landscaping service	✘
Car park	✔	Machinery	✔
Conservatories	✔	Ornaments / statues	✔
Clothing	✘	Pets / accessories	✔
Floristry	✔	Play area	✔
Garden furniture	✔	Restaurant / cafeteria	✔
Greenhouses for sale	✔	Sheds etc	✔
Houseplants	✔	Swimming pools	✘

ANSELLS GARDEN CENTRE
**High Street, Horningsea,
nr Cambridge.
Tel: (01223) 860320**

Just off the A45 (access from the eastbound carriageway), Ansells has grown over 20 years from a small nursery to one of the area's leading and most comprehensive centres. In a well spaced-out site there is all one could hope to find for a fruitful visit with the family. Garden furniture, properly displayed in a showroom, is one particularly noteable attraction, but the sundries shop is huge. Houseplants are pleasingly presented and colourful. Outside, trees and shrubs are a speciality amongst a full range of outdoor plants. At the far end is an aquatic centre and conservatory show site; to the front, a pet centre, paving centre (including ornaments) and large restaurant (Sunday lunches served), worth a visit in itself. A member of H.T.A., Ansells accepts and sells interchangeable gift tokens. The large car park is often a necessity!

*OPEN: 8:30am to 5:30pm Mon - Sat;
10:30am to 4:30pm Sundays.*

Aquatics/fish	✔	Information desk	✔
Bookshop	✔	Landscaping service	✘
Car park	✔	Machinery	✔
Conservatories	✔	Ornaments/statues	✔
Clothing	✘	Pets/accessories	✔
Floristry	✘	Play area	✘
Garden furniture	✔	Restaurant/cafeteria	✔
Greenhouses for sale	✘	Sheds etc	✔
Houseplants	✔	Swimming pools	✘

ANGLESEY ABBEY
**Lode, nr Cambridge (6 miles
north-east, signposted off A14).
Tel: (01223) 811200**

It is the many classical statues and ornaments which make this a unique garden of
the 20th century. They are to be found
scattered throughout its 100 acres of parkland, tucked away in hedged enclosures or
as part of magnificent vistas along grand
daffodil-lined avenues.

But there are less formal areas, notably
dahlia and hyacinth gardens, and some
very lovely borders in the enclosed herbaceous garden, where there's much to
delight the specialist. This leads to a river
walk (with one of the tallest wisterias
you're ever likely to see) and an old mill
house. Lord Fairhaven, and in turn the
National Trust, inherited a magnificent
collection of trees, notably limes, but
there are rarities from around the world,
such as Japanese hop hornbeam, Algerian
oak, Indian chestnut and Judas tree.

'Abbey' is something of a misnomer, for
it was actually a priory founded in 1135
(of which limited parts remain), becoming
a country house during the 17th century.
Former owners include Thomas Hobson
of 'Hobson's Choice' fame and George

Downing, founder of Downing College.
It is open to the public.

*OPEN: House 1pm to 5pm Wed - Sun
plus Bank Hol. Mons from April to mid-
October; Garden 11am to 5:30pm as
above, plus daily from mid-July to early
Sept; also RESTAURANT, SHOP & PLANT
CENTRE.*

WARESLEY PARK GARDEN CENTRE

**Waresley, nr Sandy.
(2 miles north of Gamlingay on B1040)
Tel: (01767) 650249**

From humble beginnings back in 1972 (the two small sheds can still be seen), John and Brenda Baker have built their family business into one of the area's leading centres, yet without loss of the personal touch. "Healthy plants are our strength, unusual plants our speciality" is the centre's motto. A nine-metre-wide polythene tunnel houses flowering or evergreen shrubs in winter, bedding plants and hanging baskets in the spring. An exhibition of fuchsias and geraniums in July is a popular weekend draw. The range of garden furniture is especially good, and always value-for-money. Adjacent is a light and airy coffee shop serving homemade cakes. Waresley is an agreeable little village, and you should have a very pleasant day out. The RSPB Garden is not far.

OPEN: 9am to 6pm (8pm Weds in summer) Mon - Sat; Sundays 10am to 4pm in winter, 11am to 5pm in summer. Free delivery within 20-mile radius. Facilities for disabled (incl. toilets). The management courteously offers free tea for two to visitors presenting this book.

Aquatics	✔	Information desk	✔
Bookshop	✔	Landscaping service	✘
Car park	✔	Machinery	✘
Conservatories	✔	Ornaments/statues	✔
Clothing	✘	Pets/accessories	✔
Floristry	✘	Play area	✔
Garden furniture	✔	Restaurant/cafeteria	✔
Greenhouses for sale	✔	Sheds etc	✔
Houseplants	✔	Swimming pools	✘

THE ROYAL SOCIETY FOR THE PROTECTION OF BIRDS
The Lodge, Sandy.
Tel: (01767) 680551
Fax: (01767) 692365

The RSPB's bird conservation work is well known, but not everyone is aware that its headquarters are located in these beautiful and historically important gardens in a nature reserve totalling 106 acres.

For many years the house was in the hands of the Peel family (Robert Peel founded the Police Force). The Society acquired part of the estate in 1961, and manages it on organic principles. Peat is taboo, as the RSPB campaigns vigorously to conserve peat bogs and their wildlife.

The seven acres of formal garden are distinguished by a number of features: a fine perennial border with raised balustrade teeming with butterflies in summer; Italianate columns, pergolas and old swimming pool, now stocked with Koi carp; the restored rose garden which is now the 'In Memorial' garden where benefactors may have a plaque; and a 'secret' water garden.

The estate has a number of woodland walks and nature trails. The rare natterjack toad is one inhabitant, and there are also muntjac deer, rabbits and of course, a host of wild birds including spotted flycatchers which can be found nesting in the mature wisteria and trumpet vines. There are some fine conifers including giant redwood, Douglas fir, deodar cedar and eastern hemlock, and the largest strawberry tree in the country. In spring the margins of the garden are carpeted with daffodils and bluebells under wild flowering cherry tees. There is also an azalea walk leading to a bamboo garden by a small pond where long-tailed tit usually breed.

For details of the RSPB's work and The Lodge garden please write to RSPB, The Lodge, Sandy, Bedfordshire SG19 2DL.

OPEN: nature reserve & garden daily from 9am until 9pm or sunset if earlier. SHOP/INFORMATION: 9am to 5pm weekdays, 10am to 5pm weekends & Bank Holidays. Tel: (01767) 680541.

WREST PARK HOUSE & GARDENS
Silsoe.
Tel: (01234) 262151

One of the great formal gardens of England, the 150 acres of Wrest Park are a living illustration of garden styles in vogue between 1700 and 1850. There are unmistakable French influences, both in the palatial house and in the parterre to the south, which has large flower beds, clipped hedges, fine classical statues and a vast orangery.

But most memorable is the Great Garden, with its maginificent half-mile vista from the mansion down the Long Water to the domed baroque Pavilion dating from around 1710. Flanking this expanse of water are woods in the fashion of Versailles, with intersecting avenues enriched by unexpected temples, columns and the like. Particular treasures are the Bath House (built as a romantic ruin), the Cascade Bridge and the exquisite Bowling Green House.

The estate, just under a mile from Silsoe off the A6, is now owned by English Heritage, and both house and garden are open to the public.

There are light refreshments and a shop. Special events during the summer include open-air operas, falconry, Craft Festival.

OPEN: 10am to 6pm weekends and Bank Hols, from 1st April to 30th Sept.

POPLARS NURSERY GARDEN CENTRE

Harlington Road, Toddington.
Tel: (01525) 872017
Fax: (01525) 873905

Just off junction 12 of the M1, Poplars is very accessible and well worth a journey, especially if combined with a visit to nearby Wrest Park or Luton Hoo gardens.

The display of plants, trees and shrubs is truly extensive, and chosen to suit season and locality – a key to this centre is staff's unrivalled knowledge of local conditions. The unusual is to be found alongside the staple favourites, but always in healthy condition, hence the 12-month guarantee (provided they've been properly cared for). Autumn is a good time to visit, when the 25,000 sq ft covered shopping area is transformed into a winter wonderland.

Amongst a plethora of garden things are bird tables, patio and wall construction materials, barbecues, weather vanes and sundials, but perhaps the most unusual feature is the ROYAL SCOT CRYSTAL factory shop, offering beautiful cut glass at amazingly low prices. An independent franchise, CHILTERN AQUATICS SUPERSTORE has spectacular displays of tropical and marine fish. Children will love this and the play area. The restaurant (with terrace) serves cooked meals and snacks.

Like so many of the better businesses, this one is family-run (John and Bridget Little with son David), but it is very rare in having been in the family since founded in 1901.

OPEN: 9am to 6pm Mon - Sat; 10:30am to 4:30pm Sundays. Closed Christmas & Boxing Days.

Aquatics /fish	✔	Information desk	✔
Bookshop	✔	Landscaping service	✔
Car park	✔	Machinery	✔
Conservatories	✔	Ornaments /statues	✔
Clothing	✘	Pets /accessories	✔
Floristry	✘	Play area	✔
Garden furniture	✔	Restaurant /cafeteria	✔
Greenhouses for sale	✔	Sheds etc	✔
Houseplants	✔	Swimming pools	✔

HATFIELD HOUSE
Hatfield.
Tel: (01707) 262823
Fax: (01707) 275719

The West Gardens date back to the late 15th century, but the house itself was built in the early 17th century by Robert Cecil. He employed John Tradescant the Elder to plant the gardens, and sent him all over Europe to collect specimens never before grown in Britain, including the double anemone.

The current Marchioness is undertaking a restoration to re-create the style of the 17th century. The lower West Garden has been made into a scented garden, with a herb garden at its centre. The West Garden itself, enclosed by a yew hedge, has been planted according to an early plan found in the archives, mostly with herbaceous plants, roses, irises and peonies, some quite rare. A knot garden has been formed in the courtyard, and there is also a foot maze (planted with uncommon tulips), both typical of the period.

To the south of the formal gardens lies the Wilderness Garden: 13 acres of grass, forest and ornamental trees. Rhododendrons, camellias, magnolias, cherries and flowering crab apple make spring a very colourful time here. The gravel paths are being left to grass over in order to appear more natural, and wild flowers are seeding in the grass, which is not cut until August.

Light meals are served in the RESTAURANT, and there are also attractive GIFT SHOPS and a PLANT SHOP.

Diary note: The FESTIVAL OF GARDENING is held here during the third weekend of June.

OPEN: gardens 11am to 6pm daily except Good Friday; East Gardens 2pm to 5pm Mondays only (except Bank Hols). PARK: 10:30am to 8pm daily except Good Friday. HOUSE: 1:30pm to 5pm Sundays; guided tours 12pm to 4pm Tues - Sat. Bank holiday Mons 11am to 5pm (no guided tours). Dogs not permitted to house or gardens.

NOTCUTTS GARDEN CENTRE
Hatfield Road, Smallford, St Albans.
Tel: (01727) 853224
Fax: (01727) 847251

Notcutts St Albans was the third of a family-owned chain of twelve garden centres. Since being established in 1966 it has grown to consist of all the usual departments associated with a high-class centre.

The outdoor plant sales area stocks a very wide range of hardy and not so hardy garden plants, many of which are grown by Notcutts. At the rear of the site there is a large display of conservatories and garden buildings.

The main Garden Centre building houses the garden sundries department where there is an extensive range of gardening products, as well as garden furniture and gardening equipment. Also in this building is a varied selection of foliage and flowering plants, along with a wide range of pot covers and gift items.

A children's play area is situated to the side of the furniture display area, enclosed by a lawned garden.

Historic St. Albans is only a couple of miles away so there is plenty to make a journey worthwhile. Notcutts lies on the A1057. If approaching from the A1M take

exit 3 following the A1001 towards Hatfield, then left by the Comet Hotel.

OPEN: 8:30 am to 5:30pm (5pm in winter, 6pm in summer) Mon - Sat; 11am to 5pm Sundays.

Aquatics	✔	Information desk	✔
Bookshop	✔	Landscaping service	✘
Car park	✔	Machinery (limited)	✔
Conservatories	✔	Ornaments/statues	✔
Clothing	✘	Pets/accessories	✘
Floristry	✔	Play area	✔
Garden furniture	✔	Restaurant/cafeteria	✘
Greenhouses for sale	✔	Sheds etc	✔
Houseplants	✔	Swimming pools	✘

BOOKER GARDEN CENTRE
Clay Lane, Booker, nr High Wycombe.
Tel: (01494) 532532
Fax: (01494) 520894

The story of Booker Garden Centre mirrors perfectly the development of the industry over the past 20 years or so. Its roots, back in 1972, are in a picturesque 17th-century cottage – still standing, and very much a focal point – tucked away beneath the raised banking of Wycombe Air Park (which makes for a very sheltered spot, ideal for its purpose). What

was then the paddock has, over the years, developed into much more than just a garden centre: today it is virtually a leisure and shopping complex, drawing coach parties (which are welcome) from miles around, and at peak periods even the sizeable car park is stretched to the limits. Yet it is still run by the same family and remains independent.

At 38,000 square feet, plus an additional first floor, the under cover area alone is larger than some entire centres, and is designed to be wheelchair-friendly. Every imaginable gardening accessory is to be

found beneath its vaulted roof, and some unimaginable! Among the extra attractions are a kitchen shop, whole/healthfoods shop, gym equipment, jacuzzis, toys and novelties. There's a gift wrapping service and delivery or even export can be arranged. This may be especially useful if you visit at Christmas, which is celebrated in a big way. In an extravaganza probably unmatched anywhere in the country, the display of Yuletide goodies is gargantuan, the grotto decor uninhibited, and Santa drops in by helicopter!

The original cottage still does sterling service as a bistro with a pleasant little lawn to the front. Adjacent is the aquatic studio and pet centre.

But the central purpose has not been forgotten by any means: there are plants in abundant diversity, both for garden and home, all through the year. Of special interst are a strong selection of herbs, a bonsai and exotics centre, and design and display gardens. The centre is amember of the HTA, GCA and Tourist Board.

If, after all this, you still have the time, the Blue Max Aircraft Museum is nearby.

OPEN: 9am to 6pm (8pm Wed. & Thurs.), every day.

Aquatics /fish	✔	Information desk	✔
Bookshop	✔	Landscaping service	✔
Car park	✔	Machinery	✔
Conservatories	✔	Ornaments/statues	✔
Clothing	✔	Pets/accessories	✔
Floristry	✔	Play area	✔
Garden furniture	✔	Restaurant/cafeteria	✔
Greenhouses for sale	✔	Sheds etc	✔
Houseplants	✔	Swimming pools	✔

NOTCUTTS GARDEN CENTRE & ARBORETUM

Nuneham Courtenay, nr Oxford.
Tel: (01867) 738265
Fax: (01867) 738267

There are at least three good reasons for a visit to this very attractive centre, just south of the picturesque little village of Nuneham Courtenay, close by the Golden Ball roundabout at the intersection of the A4074 with the B4015: the centre itself; the arboretum; and the lovely Mattocks rose fields nearby (see opposite).

The centre itself is pleasantly laid out on different levels – a photograph can barely do justice. Walking the paths meandering through mature planting, one could easily imagine this is indeed a splendid garden, rather than garden centre. Borders are planted up according to specific purpose – for dry or chalky soils, for example – which is as unusual as it is helpful.

As in all Notcutts centres there is an excellent stock of roses, very well displayed in containers in a large feature towards the rear of the centre, although of course this is dwarfed by the acres of bushes at nearby Mattocks. But other plants and shrubs are also very well represented, enough to satisfy the most serious gardener. One of the most colourful features is the patio section, where one can learn of ideas and products to enhance this bridge between home and garden. Garden furniture is an important facet of this, and Notcutts' range is strong on quality and is on show in the large shop along with most other garden hardware, dry goods and houseplants.

A 72-seater restaurant has an outside terrace – just the place to conclude a stimulating and enjoyable visit. And don't forget to stroll through the arboretum!

OPEN: 9am to 5:30pm (5pm Nov. to Feb.) Mon - Sat, 11am to 5pm Sundays.

Aquatics /fish	✘	Information desk	✔
Bookshop	✔	Landscaping service	✘
Car park	✔	Machinery	✘
Conservatories	✘	Ornaments /statues	✔
Clothing	✘	Pets /accessories	✘
Floristry	✘	Play area	✔
Garden furniture	✔	Restaurant /cafeteria	✔
Greenhouses for sale	✘	Sheds etc	✘
Houseplants	✔	Swimming pools	✘

MATTOCKS ROSE NURSERIES
Nuneham Courtenay, near Oxford.
Tel: (01865) 343265
Fax: (01865) 343267

The luscious fragrance from Mattock's vast rose field wafts gently over the surrounding countryside, aiding navigation, and as it bursts into view the dazzling colours cause many a sharp intake of breath. One is quite at liberty to park and explore the thousands of roses growing there, of every imaginable hue, planted in neat rows.

Catalogues are helpfully placed to assist in identification, but what they don't tell you is the interesting history behind the company. Formed by John Mattock in 1875, it has been passed on father to son right up to fourth-generation Mark Mattock today, joining the Notcutts Group in 1985. During those years the company has bred many renowned varieties, among which was a group of ground-hugging roses destined to become the forerunners of a most important development in rose cultivation.

Some 150,000 plants, of around 350 varieties, are currently grown by Mattocks, the speciality being the County Series of repeat-flowering ground cover roses. They are distributed all over Europe, and the company represents Kordes of Germany and Polsen of Denmark. All this, plus 25 gold medals in 30 years exhibiting at Chelsea, confirm the name of Mattock as of international importance, synonymous with this most versatile and prized of flowers. Founder John would be well pleased.

A short drive will take you to the Notcutts Garden Centre (see opposite), where one can puchase the roses and relax over a meal or light refreshments on the restaurant terrace.

WATERPERRY GARDENS
**Waterperry, Wheatley, nr Oxford
(just off jnctn 8 of M40).
Tel: (01844) 339254/226**

Once the practical working ground for Waterperry Horticultural School (now closed), founded by Beatrix Havergal in 1932, Waterperry may be described quite simply as a gardener's garden. The lady had a gift for training others, and the garden as the many visitors now see it is the result and furtherance of her work, today in the capable hands of Miss Mary Spiller, a former pupil.

Within the Ornamental Gardens the magnificent herbaceous border, designed by Miss Havergal, leads down through the Rock Garden, among green lawns shaded by majestic trees, to the little River Thame, a tributary of the Thames. There are shrub and heather borders, herb beds and beautfully trained fruit trees. For those interested in rock plants and alpines, Waterperry holds the National Collection of Porophyllum Saxifrages. New developments include an east-facing border full of unusual plants, a knot garden and a rose garden.

The nurseries, too, are a source of much interest; even the experienced gardener has much to learn and enjoy,

and the novice can garner a wealth of practical ideas. A wide range of quality plants, shrubs and fruits is grown and for sale in the GARDEN SHOP, which also stocks sundries, pots, tubs, bulbs and seeds, home-grown honey, books and tokens. A visit to the PEARTREE TEASHOP is a must: a choice of delicious home-made food in a relaxed atmosphere, open for morning coffee, hot and cold lunches (with wine, perhaps?), and afternoon tea.

Even those with no garden can share in and admire the order and beauty of careful cultivation. First-time visitors will find it a delight, many to return again and again for the peace and serenity in these 83 acres of unspoilt Oxfordshire.

OPEN: all year except Christmas & New Year hols,10am to 5:30pm (6pm weekends) daily from April to Sept; 10am to 4:30pm Oct. to March. Adults £2.20 pensioners £1.70, children 10-16 £1.00. Nov - Feb 75p all categories. NB: Gardens closed during 'Art in Action' July 20 - 23rd 1995.

APPLEGARTH NURSERIES
Banbury Road, Chipping Norton.
Tel: (01608) 641642

Developed from a market garden, this garden centre (member of H.T.A.) is long established. After four years working here, Duncan Birkbeck acquired the ownership in January 1993 and has continued to develop it as one of the leading centres in the area.

Well situated on the edge of the Cotswolds, and just outside Chipping Norton, Applegarth is distinguished by a comprehensive range of perennials and bedding plants, many of which are grown on site, as well as shrubs, roses, trees and conifers. The well stocked shop includes a selection of garden furniture, tools and accessories. Prominently displayed outside are stoneware and terra cotta pots alongside garden ornaments.

Most uncommonly, all key personnel are university graduates, well versed in all aspects of their profession.

OPEN: 10am to 6pm (5pm in winter), every day.

Aquatics/fish	✔	Information desk	✔
Bookshop	✘	Landscaping service	✘
Car park	✔	Machinery	✘
Conservatories	✔	Ornaments/statues	✔
Clothing	✘	Pets/accessories	✔
Floristry	✘	Play area	✘
Garden furniture	✔	Restaurant/cafeteria	✔
Greenhouses for sale	✔	Sheds etc	✔
Houseplants	✔	Swimming pools	✘

BARNSLEY HOUSE GARDEN

Barnsley, nr Cirencester.
Tel: (01285) 740281
Fax: (01285) 740628

Recipient of Christie's and the HHA's Award for the Best Garden in 1988, Barnsley is one of England's most famous gardens. This is in part due to the series of widely read gardening books by the owner, Rosemary Verey, as well as numerous magazine articles and television appearances, but it is the imaginative and quality planting which earns a place in the front rank.

This acclaim is all the more extraordinary when one is aware that the garden comprises just four acres. At the centre stands the lovely mellow honey-stone Cotswolds house (not open), built in 1697. The garden has been designed around it, so that there is a series of areas, rather than enclosures, defined by pathways leading on to new surprises. Contemporary fashions, such as the celebrated kitchen and knot gardens, were revived and the result is a wonderfully harmonious blend of patterns, form and colour, a joy to behold even in winter. Herbaceous planting is especially effective, and there are also a laburnam walk, herb garden, 18th-century summer

houses, temples and statues.

Many interesting plants are for sale, plus teak garden furniture, Italian sun umbrellas, antiques, books and cards. The recommended Village Pub is just yards away.

OPEN: 10am to 6pm, Mon Wed, Thurs & Sat throughout the year. Parties and coaches by appointment. Guided tour by Rosemary Verey herself can be arranged for an extra fee.

WESTONBIRT PLANT CENTRE & ARBORETUM

Tetbury, near Gloucester.
Tel: (01666) 880544
Fax: (01666) 880559

Of considerable international importance, Westonbirt is home to some 18,000 trees, planted from 1829 in 600 exquisitely landscaped acres, belonging to the Forestry Commission since 1956. Visitors can wander at will through 17 miles of trails, or just sit in a leafy glade admiring some of the world's tallest, oldest and rarest trees and shrubs.

Every season has its own magic when there are so many trees to mark its passing. Autumn is, of course, spectacular, but in a fall of winter snow, or even just a heavy frost, the arboretum becomes a place of profound stillness and beauty. Spring sees magnificent displays of rhododendrons, azaleas, magnolias and the wild flowers of Silkwood. In summer, stroll lazily down Lime Avenue watching the butterflies skip. You may even spot deer or badger. Whatever the time of year, Westonbirt is truly unforgetable, an oasis of tranquility.

It will not surprise you to know that the adjacent PLANT CENTRE specialises very much in trees and shrubs, but it also stocks seeds, composts, perennials, alpines, houseplants, books and much more, including expert advice. Although the range is outstanding, the centre has a unique order service, and will try to obtain any plant for you, however rare.

At the VISITOR CENTRE you will find information, maps and guides, an exhibition and video programme, a first rate country gift shop and courtyard cafe serving tasty food. There are also two picnic areas, one dog-free. An education officer is on hand and there are two equipped classrooms – special rates for schools and colleges which book ahead. Enquiries welcome.

OPEN: Daily throughout the year from 10am to 8pm or sunset if earlier. Entry fee payable. Limited number of wheelchairs available - best reserve in advance. Westonbirt lies just a few miles to the south west of Tetbury.

HIGHFIELD NURSERIES

Bristol Road, Whitminster, nr Gloucester.
Tel: (01452) 741444
Fax: (01452) 740750

More than just a garden centre, Highfield provides something for all the family. A wide selection of trees, shrubs, herbaceous and roses for the discerning gardener is backed up by Highfield's 80-page full colour catalogue. Fruit trees and fruiting plants are specialities, and the choice considerably exceeds that of most centres. Knowledgeable staff are always on hand to give advice.

A large pet centre is very popular, with its small animals, reptiles, birds and large aquatic centre. Cane furniture, designer clothing at affordable prices, and a large selection of beautiful silk flowers are just a few of the other great attractions.

Aquatics/fish	✔	Information desk	✔
Bookshop	✔	Landscaping service	✔
Car park	✔	Machinery	✘
Conservatories	✔	Ornaments/statues	✔
Clothing	✔	Pets/accessories	✔
Floristry	✔	Play area	✘
Garden furniture	✔	Restaurant/cafeteria	✔
Greenhouses for sale	✔	Sheds etc	✔
Houseplants	✔	Swimming pools	✘

The sizeable coffee shop serves morning coffee, delicious home-made cakes, lunches and afternoon teas.

Mail order was the mainstay of the business, started in 1920, and the nursery continues to grow most of the plants for the centre. Visitors are welcome at the nearby NURSERY Mon – Fri, 9am to 5pm. (Just a half-mile from junction 13 of the M5, the Centre is in an ideal position to welcome visitors from afar.) Highfield's credentials as a 'serious' garden centre are witnessed by membership of the Nuclear Stock Association, East Malling Research Station and the Horticultural Trades Association.

OPEN: 9am to 6pm Mon - Sat; 10:30am to 4:30pm Suns; closed Christmas Day & Boxing Day.

Joan Greenway, son Tim and Trevor Wellington are the owners.

HIDCOTE MANOR GARDEN
Chipping Campden.
Tel: (01386) 438333

The useful map and guide lists 28 features – courtyards, gardens, terraces, borders – which indicate the structured nature of this unique and highly influential garden, one of the very best known in Britain. With its hedged rooms linked by corridors and furnished with all kinds of topiary, Hidcote is redolent of the 'Old English' style favoured by the late Victorians, and also hints at the French connections of its creator, the enigmatic Lawrence Johnston, who began work in 1907.

Lavish colour interspersed with relative simplicity make for greater impact as one progresses through the 'rooms.' Were it in a house, the Theatre Lawn would surely be the ballroom; open-air theatre is performed here during the summer. The Old Garden, dominated by a cedar of Lebanon, was the first to be planted, and its borders reflect Gertrude Jekyll's principles of subtlety of colour and form. From there one moves on to the White Garden, full of all types of white flowers; there are the Red Borders, the Winter Border, the Fuchsia Garden, Bathing Pool Garden, Poppy Garden, three Stream Gardens, Pine Garden, Rose Borders, a Kitchen Garden and too much else to be detailed here. Special mention should go to Mrs Winthrop's Garden, named after Johnston's mother (with whom he lived for much of his life): the colour scheme here is yellow through to lime green, with strong dark blue for contrast.

In short, Hidcote is a must for any garden-lover. It is situated four miles north-east of Chipping Campden (sign-posted from the B4632). It also has a licensed RESTAURANT, PLANT SHOP, and NATIONAL TRUST SHOP.

OPEN: 11am to 7pm (last admission 6pm or 1 hour before sunset if earlier) daily except Tues & Fri, from April to the end of October. Closed Good Friday. Parties by written appointment. No picnics, games or dogs.

UPTON HOUSE
nr Banbury.
Tel: (01295) 670266

At 700 feet this must be one of southern England's highest stately homes. Its beautiful garden falls away steeply in a series of terraces and combes, quite a sight to behold from the surrounding hills. To the left of the lawn in front of the house is a rock garden, then a path flanked by herbaceous borders heads down towards a pond, near which is a dream of a kitchen garden. A small rose garden is enclosed by yew hedges, and for a neighbour has a small informal garden. This sector of the grand scheme is a tapestry of colour from early spring until late summer.

To the west another deep combe contains three 17th-century square ponds, created by damming the stream. Only the middle still exists and has goldfish; the upper is now an orchard of flowering cherries, the lower a bog garden. There are many unusual plants, especially perennials, to be found throughout, and Upton is home to the National Collection of Asters.

The house itself, completed in 1695 by the unlikely-named Sir Rushout Cullen, is of considerable importance. An outstanding collection of paintings includes works by El Greco, Breughel, Bosch, Memling, Guardi, Hogarth and Stubbs; also Brussels tapestries, Sevres porcelain and Chelsea figures. TEA ROOM and NATIONAL TRUST SHOP. Upton is on the A422, 12 miles south-east of Stratford-on-Avon.

OPEN: 2pm to 6pm (last admissions 5:30) Sat - Wed, incl. Bank Hol. Mons, from 1st April to 31st Oct. Parties by written appointment. No sharp-heeled shoes or photography in house. No dogs. Motorised buggy with driver available for access to lower garden.

PACKWOOD HOUSE
Lapworth, nr Solihull.
Tel: (01564) 782024

Legend has it that Charles II took refreshment at Packwood after his defeat at Worcester in 1651. History does not record whether he found time to stroll in the gardens, but if he did then he may have witnessed the beginnings of the famous Yew Garden, said to represent the Sermon on the Mount ("Blessed are the peace makers" would be most apposite). Established by John Fetherston, whose family continued to live here until 1869, it is a quite extraordinary topiary, with a 'multitude', 12 'Apostles' and 'The Master'. It's a nice idea, but there is evidence to suggest that this theme was really the product of the19th century.

What is not in dispute is that Packwood today is a fine 16th-century house and lovely garden, set in the Forest of Arden but not far from the suburban sprawl of Birmingham (2 miles east of Hockley Heath, signposted off A3400). A splendid wrought iron gate connects the Yew Garden to a wide terraced walk bordered by flowers. On the south face of the terrace may be seen bee boles, clearly shown on plans dated 1756. At the other end of this walk is the Sunken Garden, which has a pool and glorious borders of summer colour. To the north-west side of the house, again surrounded by a yew hedge, is a cold plunge bath dating from 1680. The house itself has much worth seeing, including a connoisseur's collection of furniture, tapestries and needlework.

There is also a NATIONAL TRUST SHOP, and another NT property, Baddesley Clinton, is just 2 miles.

OPEN: 2pm to 6pm Wed - Sun plus Bank Hol. Mons, from April to end of Sept (closed Good Friday); 12:30pm to 4:30pm Wed - Sun during October. Last admissions half-hour before closing. Parties by written appointment. Picnics in avenue opp. house. No sharp-heeled shoes in house.

NOTCUTTS GARDEN CENTRE
Stratford Road, Shirley, nr Solihull.
Tel: 0121 744 4501
Fax: 0121 745 4867

The cathedral-like dome is a local landmark and can easily be seen from quite a distance – appropriate enough for this furthermost outpost of the excellent Notcutts empire. Beneath this light and airy canopy is to be found an attractive water feature, outstanding range of giftware, exclusive garden furniture, a wide choice of houseplants, a splendid 160-seater licensed restaurant and much more.

In the six acres outside lies a tremendous variety of plant stock – over 2,000 types. But not only plants: you will also discover an exceptionally good range of pots and ornaments, hanging baskets and patio section, all immaculately laid out and easy to follow, in such a way as it is bound to generate ideas. Nursery stock is home grown. Greenhouses, conservatories and sheds are franchised.

Christmas is a very special time here: the dome is decked out in full regalia, capturing the magic of the season – unforgettable for children and adults alike.

So, make the short detour off the motorway and home in on the dome for a very pleasant and productive hour or two.

OPEN: 9am to 6pm Mon -Sat; 11am to 5pm Sundays.

Aquatics	✔	Information desk	✔
Bookshop	✔	Landscaping service	✔
Car park	✔	Machinery	✔
Conservatories	✔	Ornaments/statues	✔
Clothing (limited)	✔	Pets/accessories	✘
Floristry	✘	Play area	✔
Garden furniture	✔	Restaurant/cafeteria	✔
Greenhouses for sale	✔	Sheds etc	✔
Houseplants	✔	Swimming pools	✘

GUESTS FOR PLANTS LTD
Queens Road Nurseries, Kenilworth.
Tel: (01926) 52759

A town centre site like this does offer the advantage that one could easily combine a visit with a shopping trip. The entrance is right by the Tut'n'Shive pub, which could also be very handy. Ryton Organic Gardens are just a few minutes drive, as is historically important Kenilworth Castle.

Maximum use is made of limited space: plants are positioned in neat rows and labelling could hardly be bettered, eg Red Shrubs; White Shrubs; Yellow Shrubs; 8ft plus, Herbs for Cooking, etc. Behind this is a good display of ornamental stoneware and large wooden water barrels and pumps. To one side are rows of fruit trees next to the houseplants greenhouse, but it is the outstanding selection of bedding plants, grown on the premises, sheltered in rows of concrete frames and available all through the season, which is the centre's most exceptional feature.

An astonishing amount is also packed into the shop, including strimmers, wild bird seed and tables, dried flowers, tools, a book rack and much else. Behind the desk are photos of the helpful staff, including manager Les Beard and owner Andrew Guest. They work for a family

company (member of HTA) which has now been established for 60 years – eloquent enough testimony.

OPEN: 9am (10am Sundays) to 5:30pm every day.

Aquatics	✔	Information desk	✔
Bookshop (rack)	✘	Landscaping service	✔
Car park	✔	Machinery (limited)	✔
Conservatories	✘	Ornaments/statues	✔
Clothing	✘	Pets/accessories	✘
Floristry	✘	Play area	✘
Garden furniture	✘	Restaurant/cafeteria	✘
Greenhouses for sale	✘	Sheds etc	✘
Houseplants	✔	Swimming pools	✘

RYTON ORGANIC GARDENS

Ryton on Dunsmore, nr Coventry.
Tel: (01203) 303517
Fax: (01203) 639229

Viewers of Channel 4's "All Muck and Magic" will know that Ryton was the setting for the series. Director Jackie Gear is also a TV and Radio presenter, and an author on the subject of organic gardening. Although now a major tourist attraction, these gardens (run by The Henry Doubleday Research Association) have a serious purpose: to show that 'environment-friendly' gardening is not just a passing fad but a realistic and very desirable way of achieving the best results.

The 10 beautiful acres contain formal rose gardens, ornamentals, alpine banks, shrub borders, colourful flower beds, a wildflower meadow (recapturing the age before chemical sprays) and conservation area. Special mention must go to the wonderful vegetables and soft fruits, many of which find their way to the tables of the celebrated restaurant, recommended by Egon Ronay and other good food guides.

The 'muck' which provides the 'magic' comes courtesy of the Rare Breeds collection, with the bonus that the animals are a delight to children (spring and summer months only). The latter also have a climbing frame and toddlers' pit, but the latest big attraction is a replica Swiss chalet, complete to every detail, including an upstairs balcony.

The shop sells a wide range of organic food and wine, comprehensive selection of organic gardening books and garden products, including ornaments and clothing. A good number of organic herbs, alpines, perennials and fruit trees are also sold, plus fresh flowers. There's also an Education Centre which may be hired for conferences etc or even a highly original wedding reception! A full calendar of special events may be obtained from the information desk.

OPEN: 10am to 6pm daily from March to Sept, 10am to 4pm Oct - Feb. Closed during Christmas week.

KIRBY HALL
nr Corby.
Tel: (01536) 203230

Suddenly emerging out of the rolling countryside (just four miles north-east of industrial Corby), the Hall is a stirring and spectacular sight, especially when the late afternoon sun illuminates the mellow stonework. Clearly, this was a Renaissance house of some grandeur (it was built for Christopher Hatton, one of Queen Elizabeth's favourites), but is now a part-ruin. Neverthless, many of the rooms can be explored, and the richly carved stonework is still there to be discovered.

English Heritage is restoring both house and garden, probably the most important project of its kind in the country. The garden is regaining its spectacular baroque design of the late 17th century, and this 20th-century 'Renaissance' will be fascinating to witness.

A programme of special events includes the likes of open-air operas, a craft festival, antiques fair and Shakespeare plays – in a truly memorable setting.

OPEN: 10am to 6pm daily from 1st April to 31st October; 10am to 4pm Wed - Sun from 1st Nov. to 31st March.

HILL FARM HERBS
Park Walk, Brigstock, nr Kettering.
Tel: (01536) 373694
Fax: (01536) 373246

There has been a surge of interest in herbs in recent years, not just for the kitchen but also for medicinal, aromatic and dying purposes. At the forefront of this trend is Hill Farm Herbs (HTA), established in 1987 by Eileen and Mike Simpson in this agreeable village, and signposted off the A6116 Corby to Thrapston road.

Located at the back of an old stone farmhouse, they grow an ever-increasing range of herbs and cottage garden plants. It is a pleasure to browse through the garden areas, some planted informally, others according to usage (Cook's Garden, for example), but always tantalising the senses.

There's more temptation in the several 'barn shops' on site: the Herb Shop sells seeds, pot-pourris, essential oils, cosmetics, scented candles, books, cards and posters; the Flower Room stocks a large choice of dried flowers and herbs, as well as many pretty accessories. The new Farm Pantry has traditional preserves, home-made herb vinegars, dried herbs and spices, herbal teas and diverse kitchenware, and there's also a good selection of terra cotta pots which can be planted to customers' requirements. The TEA SHOP is open from Easter to the end of September.

OPEN: 10:30am to 5:30pm (4:30pm in winter) every day except Christmas & Boxing Days. Catalogue produced and mail order service. Party visits can be arranged.

COTTESBROOKE HALL

Cottesbrooke, nr Northampton.
Tel: (01604) 505808
Fax: (01604) 505619

Often considered to be the pattern for Jane Austen's 'Mansfield Park', Cottesbrooke is a prime example of how to marry house with gardens. The former is of the Queen Anne period (1702) while the latter, formal and wild, have been developed mostly during this century. A number of distinguished landscapers have been involved: Edward Schulz in the early years, Sir Geoffrey Jellicoe before World War II, Dame Sylvia Crowe afterwards. Inspiration came principally from the late Hon. Lady Macdonald-Buchanan.

The more notable garden features include to the south the Forecourt, a formal garden designed by Jellicoe and commanding superb vistas from the lawn; the Statue Walk to the west, where you will also find the Spinney and Pool Gardens; nearer the house is the Dutch or Time Garden and the Terrace with its lovely herbaceous borders, backed by two magnificent Cedars of Lebanon of around the same age as the house. A short walk across the park brings you to the Wild Gardens (east and west divided by the Hunter's Bridge), through which runs a brook crossed by stepping stones. The acers here are especially fine in spring and autumn, and the banks of rhododendrons and azaleas are a small miracle given the nature of the soil. A herb garden is a recent addition.

The house, too, has much of beauty and interest, including the Woolavington Collection of sporting pictures (perhaps the finest in Europe), exceptional wrought iron work and Rococo papier mache wall decoration.

Refreshments are available in the tearooms and unusual plants are for sale.

OPEN: 2pm to 5:30pm (last admission 5pm) Thursdays from 20th April to 28th September, plus Easter Monday, May Day, Spring Bank Holiday, August Bank Holiday. Parties accommodated by appointment on other days.

PLANTSMAN
**West Haddon Nurseries,
Northampton Road, West Haddon.
Tel & Fax: (01788) 510206**

Northamptonshire proclaims itself "Rose of the Shires" and has indeed long been a county strong on horticulture. It was on these old market garden premises that Mike and Dave Davis, father and son as partners, founded Plantsman (member of HTA) in 1990. They have fast acquired a following from all around the surrounding area.

This not being an overly large centre, they can afford to give each customer personal service, based on years of practical gardening experience. Their range of plants, bulbs and seeds is nevertheless truly comprehensive, but the speciality is assuredly high quality herbaceous plants, including many uncommon varieties. Two large beds of approx. 80ft by 20ft are laid out as herbaceous borders, and feature a sizeable lily pond and ornamental surround. There are also a wide choice of houseplants in a large greenhouse, a good sundries shop and shrub sales beds.

It may be handy to know that the centre has a Teleflorist service, if you suddenly realise you've forgotten an anniversary.

Aquatics	✔	Information desk	✘
Bookshop	✘	Landscaping service	✘
Car park	✔	Machinery	✔
Conservatories	✘	Ornaments/statues	✔
Clothing	✘	Pets/accessories	✘
Floristry	✔	Play area	✘
Garden furniture	✘	Restaurant/cafeteria	✘
Greenhouses for sale	✔	Sheds etc	✔
Houseplants	✔	Swimming pools	✘

*OPEN: 9am to 5:30pm Mon - Sat;
10am - 5:30pm Sundays, throughout
the year.*

DEANE & AMOS LTD (CONSERVATORIES)
12/13 North Portway Close
Round Spinney, Northampton.
Tel: (01604) 647121
Fax: (01604) 790401

For more than 20 years this family business has been designing and crafting the very finest of conservatories, and in doing so has enhanced the character and ambience of many a home.

The service includes responsibility for every aspect of the project, from quotation to completion. Once a design has been agreed and materials chosen, the base and building work is carried out under supervision while the company's own factory produces the superstructure ready for installation on site.

The materials used are of the best quality: high-strength PVCu, available in white, brown or woodgrain mahogany effect; traditional hardwod; powder-coated aluminium. All glazing is to current British Standards, brick and stone is carefully matched to existing buildings, and there is wide range of floor finishes, including Italian ceramic tiles.

A conservatory will transform and add value to your home, increasing its warmth, comfort and living space.

Their success means they are now operating outside of Northants, so telephone or call at their showroom, or visit the new

show site at COUNTRY GARDENS, HARLESTONE HEATH GARDEN CENTRE, Harlestone Road, Northampton,
tel: (0604) 588153.

Open every day from 10am to 5pm.